In the Mind's Eye

Advanced Curriculum From Vanderbilt University's Programs for Talented Youth

In the Mind's Eye

Truth Versus Perception

ELA Lessons for Gifted and Advanced Learners in Grades 6–8

Emily Mofield, Ed.D.,
& Tamra Stambaugh, Ph.D.

PRUFROCK PRESS INC.

WACO, TEXAS

Edited by Katy McDowall

Cover design by Raquel Trevino and layout design by Allegra Denbo

Cover image: Gogh, Vincent van (1853-1890). Self Portrait. 1887. Oil on canvas, 44.1 x 35.1 cm. Image copyright © Musee d'Orsay. Photo Credit: Erich Lessing / Art Resource, NY. (ARTI20709)

ISBN-13: 978-1-61821-482-9

Prufrock Press Inc.
P.O. Box 8813
Waco, TX 76714-8813
Phone: (800) 998-2208
Fax: (800) 240-0333
http://www.prufrock.com

Table of Contents

Dedication

To Ashley, Ellie, and my parents, for your sacrificial love.
—Emily

To my nieces and nephews and other gifted students I have worked with who need an accelerated curriculum to stay engaged and to grow in their learning.
—Tamra

Acknowledgements

We would like express heartfelt gratitude to those dedicated administrators and teachers who implemented the lessons and provided valuable feedback for revisions. You know who you are and we are most grateful! We especially want to recognize Emilie Hall for organizing data and fine-tuning lessons during the editing process. Dr. Elizabeth Covington is appreciated for her professional insight into the development of the literary and rhetorical analysis models to verify the scholarly validity of their use. We also appreciate the work of our editor, Katy McDowall, for her steadfast work and patience as we continued to hone lessons and ask questions well into the editing process. Finally, we are honored to build these lessons on a solid foundation of knowledge, theory, and best practices in gifted education and curriculum development established from the inspiring work of Dr. Joyce VanTassel-Baska.

Introduction

In the Mind's Eye: Truth Versus Perception is designed specifically with gifted and high-achieving middle and early high school learners in mind. These concept-based lessons are accelerated beyond typical grade-level standards and include advanced models and organizers to help students analyze a variety of texts. The unit invites students on a philosophical exploration of the themes of truth and perception. Lessons include a major emphasis on rigorous evidence-based discourse through the study of common themes and content-rich, challenging informational and fictional texts. The unit applies concepts from Plato's "Allegory of the Cave" to guide students in discovering how reality is presented and interpreted in fiction, nonfiction, art, and media. Students engage in activities such as Socratic seminars, literary analyses, skits, art projects, and creative writing to understand differing perceptions of reality. Lessons include close readings with text-dependent questions, choice-based differentiated products, rubrics, formative assessments, and ELA tasks that require students to analyze texts for rhetorical features, literary elements, and themes through argument, explanatory, and prose-constructed writing. The unit features art from M. C. Escher and Vincent Van Gogh, short stories from Guy de Maupassant and Shirley Jackson, longer texts by Daniel Keyes and Ray Bradbury, and informational texts related to sociology, Nazi propaganda, and Christopher Columbus. Aligned to the Common Core State Standards (CCSS), this unit encourages students to translate learning to real-world contexts and problems by exploring themes of disillusionment, social deception, and the power of perception.

CONCEPTUAL FRAMEWORK

In the Mind's Eye: Truth Versus Perception is one of four units designed specifically for gifted middle school students (grades 6–8) to support the acquisition of textual analysis skills including identifying the relationship between literary elements within a text, evaluating arguments, enhancing thinking and communication skills, and connecting conceptual generalizations from cross-curricular themes through a variety of media including literary texts, art, and primary source documents. The Integrated Curriculum Model (ICM; VanTassel-Baska, 1986) is the conceptual framework used for the unit design. Components of the framework are embedded in each lesson: accelerated content, advanced literacy processes of the discipline (e.g., rhetorical analysis and literary analysis), and conceptual understandings. For example, the accelerated content includes ELA (English language arts) standards, aligned to the CCSS. The CCSS selected for each unit are above the grade level(s) for which the unit was intended. Each unit also includes process skills and specific models to help students evaluate the development of effective arguments; analyze a variety of texts, art, and primary sources; and connect literature to real-world applications (see Appendices A and B for more information on the models). The content of each lesson is connected by an overarching theme and key generalizations that span a variety of disciplines. These concepts vary by unit and include power, truth versus perception, individuality versus conformity, and freedom. Table 1 shows how each unit in this series aligns with the ICM features. The ICM model was selected based on its evidence-supported success in increasing gifted student achievement (see VanTassel-Baska & Stambaugh, 2008).

INTENDED GRADE LEVEL(S)

It is well known in gifted education that accelerated content is essential for increasing the academic achievement and social-emotional growth of gifted students (Assouline, Colangelo, VanTassel-Baska, & Lupkowski-Shoplik, 2015; Colangelo, Assouline, & Gross, 2004; Steenbergen-Hu, & Moon, 2011). This unit is intended for and has been piloted with gifted students in grades 6–8. The unit is aligned to CCSS standards primarily focused on grades 9–10 with some lower grade standards included as needed. The accelerated content is necessary so that gifted students have the opportunity to gain new language arts content knowledge at a pace and level that is appropriate for their learning needs. Gifted students' readiness and experience levels vary, as do their abilities. Because school contexts and content emphases are different, it is up to each teacher to determine which unit is best suited for his or her particular students and at which grade levels. Some gifted students may find this unit engaging as a sixth grader while others may need to wait until grade 7 or 8 to fully participate and understand the unit concepts. Teachers of 9th and 10th graders may find that these units are on target for many of their general education students.

Table 1
The Integrated Curriculum Model Alignment by Unit

Unit	Accelerated Content	Advanced Processes Models/Organizers	Concept/Generalizations
Finding Freedom	Aligned to grade 9 and 10 CCSS standards	Advanced Models: ■ Social Studies Connections ■ Rhetorical Analysis Organizers: ■ Reasoning About a Situation or Event ■ Big Idea Reflection: Primary Sources	■ Freedom requires sacrifice. ■ Freedom requires responsibility. ■ Freedom is threatened by internal and external forces.
Perspectives of Power	Aligned to grade 9 and 10 CCSS standards	Advanced Models: ■ Literary Analysis ■ Visual Analysis ■ Rhetorical Analysis Organizers: ■ Big Idea Reflection ■ Reasoning About a Situation or Event	■ Power is the ability to influence. ■ Power is connected to a source. ■ Power may be used or abused.
I, Me, You, We: Individuality Versus Conformity	Aligned to grade 9 and 10 CCSS standards	Advanced Models: ■ Literary Analysis ■ Visual Analysis ■ Rhetorical Analysis Organizers: ■ Big Idea Reflection ■ Reasoning About a Situation or Event	■ Both conformity and individuality are agents of change. ■ Both conformity and individuality involve sacrifice. ■ There are positives and negatives to both conformity and individuality.
In the Mind's Eye: Truth Versus Perception	Aligned to grade 9 and 10 CCSS standards	Advanced Models: ■ Literary Analysis ■ Visual Analysis ■ Rhetorical Analysis Organizers: ■ Big Idea Reflection ■ Reasoning About a Situation or Event	■ Perception of truth varies. ■ There are negatives and positives in realizing the truth. ■ There are consequences to believing perception rather than the truth.

LESSON FORMAT AND GUIDELINES

Each lesson in this unit follows a similar format for ease of use. Teachers select from a variety of questions, activities, and differentiated products to best meet their students' needs.

Alignment to Standards

The unit incorporates the key pedagogical shifts highlighted as part of the CCSS. For example, students read both literary and informational texts from a variety of sources and perspectives. Through the use of primary sources, they learn domain-specific content from their readings and are required to provide text-based evidence to support their answers or ideas. Each lesson also supports opportunities for students to make or analyze an argument, defend a position, or interpret a text. Of course, part of close reading and understanding of a text includes the use of domain-specific vocabulary. The readings selected throughout the unit build upon specific concepts and highlight multiple perspectives. Many readings use vocabulary of the time period or a specific discipline, for which students must understand and define.

The beginning of each lesson includes a list of the overarching goals and objectives as well as CCSS specific to each lesson. The end of the unit includes a CCSS alignment chart (p. 229). This unit was not designed to meet every CCSS ELA standard for a particular grade level.

Materials

When differentiating for the gifted, it is important for the materials and readings to be at a level commensurate with the student's ability. The readings and resources in this unit have been carefully selected and include either sophisticated concepts or reading selections above most middle school grade levels. The materials section includes a list of resources needed for the lesson. Some of the listed materials are optional and many of the selected texts, visuals, or videos are readily available online as a free download. When possible, reliable sites and specific links, available at the time of this unit's printing, are provided. *A word of caution:* It is important to note that some of the readings may be controversial or contain advanced or sensitive concepts and content. A cautionary note is provided in lessons with the most controversial issues. Still, it is up to the teacher and school administration to understand the context of his or her district and to determine whether or not a reading or discussion is appropriate or whether a different text or discussion-based question should be used. As the lessons follow a specific format and the analysis models can be used with any text, teachers may easily substitute a more appropriate source and then apply questions and activities for that source using a selected analysis model as a guide (see Appendix A for specific descriptions of each model).

Introductory Activities

The introductory activities provide a real-world connection or "hook" that sets the tone for the remainder of the lesson and enhances student engagement. Sample options include quick debates about an issue or dilemma, symbol designs to illustrate a key concept or idea, or key discussion questions that help students better understand the relevance of a lesson's text, art, or primary source.

Text-Dependent Questions for Close Reading

This section provides questions that ensure students understand the text. These close reading questions are varied and the majority focus on comprehension and inference making. Students are to answer these questions using textual evidence. Note that prediction or speculation questions that cannot be supported with evidence from the text are not appropriate for this section. A variety of questions are listed, but not all questions should be asked in a given lesson. Instead, teachers select four to six questions from the list for students to discuss in small groups, Socratic seminars, or as an entire class. Of course, if students are struggling to understand the text, additional questions or background information may be required. The questions in this section are *not* intended as homework or to be responded to in writing on a consistent basis. These questions are designed for discussion purposes so that teachers can check for understanding and help students support new ideas or clarify misunderstandings.

Analysis Section

This is the most comprehensive and complex section of each lesson and includes a variety of advanced processes and specific models so that students make real-world connections to big ideas and better analyze literature, rhetorical arguments, and visual prompts. These models were created after extensive research and consultation with an English language arts expert to ensure content validity. See Appendix A for a detailed explanation, instructions, and an example lesson using each model.

When implementing the unit, it is recommended that each model be presented in its entirety at least three times, with emphasis given to the literary analysis and rhetorical analysis models. Teachers are encouraged to use the complex features of the models, as these add depth and complexity to the unit content and encourage gifted students to think about the relationships between key ideas in more sophisticated ways. It is at the teacher's discretion to determine which model(s) are to be used for each lesson based upon students' interest, level of understanding, and engagement.

In-Class Activities to Deepen Learning

The activities included here provide hands-on or thought-provoking ideas that support or solidify student learning. Tasks incorporate real-world connections and include issue-based questions linked to a big idea, quick debates about an issue, or technology extensions. These activities also include opportunities for self-reflection on how the lesson content impacted their learning. One or all of the activities in this section may be taught.

Concept Connections

The concept connections section focuses on the third component of the ICM. The purpose of this section is to help students see the relationships between different texts and perspectives as these relate to key generalizations about truth versus perception. A graphic organizer comprised of the conceptual generalizations and key unit readings is provided in the unit to help students organize their ideas and determine patterns among the various readings. It is important to refer to the concept generalizations in each lesson, even if the concept chart is not completed for every reading.

Choice-Based Differentiated Products

Several choice-based differentiated products are also part of each lesson. Students may select one of the choice products to showcase their strengths and individual understanding or, if pressed for time, teachers may require two or three choice-based products for students to complete during the course of the unit. The options listed allow students an opportunity to pursue their interests and to gain a deeper understanding of a learning objective as they present their understanding in a creative way. Differentiated products vary by lesson and may include investigating a real-world problem, designing visuals, applying an advanced model to other related sources, writing essays, and developing products or presentations for an audience. Rubrics are provided in Appendix C to guide product creation and teacher feedback. The rubrics may also be used for peer and self-evaluations.

ELA Practice Tasks

Designed with the CCSS assessments in mind, the ELA practice tasks support the writing and argument analysis items typically assessed as part of a state assessment. The ELA tasks incorporate multiple standards and require complex thinking. Students are asked to respond to a prompt by creating a well-developed essay in which they create or analyze arguments, critique texts, explain an issue from multiple perspectives, or explain the development of key concepts presented in a text. It is at the teacher's discretion to determine how many ELA practice tasks students should write throughout the course of the unit. Although not explicitly stated in the unit, teachers are encouraged to model the writing process, help students analyze exemplars and inappropriate responses, and provide individual feedback.

Formative Assessment

The formative assessment section focuses on assessing a student's understanding of a single-faceted objective such as making inferences or determining how an author used a literary element to convey an idea or theme. A rubric is included with each prompt so that teachers can quickly assess responses, provide feedback, and determine next steps in their students' learning. Questions require a written response of no more than a paragraph. The formative assessments may be used to determine the extent to which students understand the meaning of a text and can provide supporting evidence and target instruction based on individual needs. Teachers may require students to complete an ELA practice task in one lesson and a formative assessment task in another so that students' thinking and understanding can be measured in a variety of ways.

Handouts

Following each lesson, all necessary handouts for lesson completion are included (e.g., readings, visuals, organizers, blank analysis models, and other sources not readily available online). As previously stated in the materials section, sometimes teachers are led to specific web-based links or it is recommended that popular sources be found online. This is especially important for featured art (which doesn't copy well) and popularized primary sources and texts. Any source that is essential to the lesson or is difficult to access is included as a handout.

Other Unit Features

This unit includes a culminating lesson that synthesizes many of the learning objectives into a comprehensive project so that students may showcase their learning in a creative way. These options may include the application of the advanced content learned throughout the unit, real-world problem solving, and the development of authentic products. Additionally, the culminating lesson includes in-depth self-reflections that guide students to relate their own lives to concept-themes.

Rubrics are provided so that students understand the expectations of a task and teachers can easily analyze student products given set criteria. The rubrics are also useful for peer and self-evaluations.

Teacher background information is another feature found in many lessons, especially those with more complicated texts. Although some background information is provided, teachers are encouraged to study specific literary analysis critiques for a particular reading, research the history of a specific primary source (if not already known), and seek varied interpretations of the text or visual. Online links to literary critiques are provided for some lessons, when appropriate.

Sample responses are also included for many complex questions and analysis models. It is important to understand that the answers provided are a guide and should not be construed as the only correct response. Student answers will vary and many unanticipated responses may be correct. Teachers are encouraged to use the provided answers to better understand the intent of the question, to model how to arrive at an appropriate response, to demonstrate how to use a specific analysis model, and to familiarize themselves with the intent of a particular passage.

Finally, this unit features instructions for using models, sample lessons, blank model handouts, and guides to support students' thinking about each element of a given analysis model. Rubrics are also provided to assess student products and responses. Specifically, Appendix A highlights instructions, handouts, and examples for each analysis model. Appendix B includes blank models and guides for thinking about each element of a particular model, and Appendix C includes rubrics for assessing student progress.

Time Allotment

Most lessons can be taught within 90–120 minutes, although some lessons may take longer. The length of the lesson also depends upon how many models and activities are employed, how interested students are in a particular issue or text, and how many times a text needs to be read or analyzed for students to gain understanding. In general, it is anticipated that this unit can be taught with approximately 45 hours of instruction time if teachers follow the recommended guidelines as reported in this section.

Differentiation

Gifted students are a heterogeneous group and their ability levels, pace of learning, interests, and depth of understanding vary. Although this unit was written with gifted middle school students in mind, differentiation is still necessary. A variety of differentiated opportunities are embedded in the unit, such as choice-based product options, open-ended questions, and more simple and complex ways to adapt the analysis models and adjust instruction based on students' readiness and interest levels.

The "choice-based differentiated products" section in each lesson allows students to select a task of interest and to showcase their learning in a way that best meets their individual preferences and learning styles. In addition, the final lesson synthesizes unit goals and provides opportunities for students to select a project of their own choosing to explore in depth. The close reading questions can also be differentiated. Teachers may assign specific questions to individual students or groups of students based on their responses from formative assessments or ELA tasks.

The ELA process models (e.g., literary analysis, rhetorical analysis, and big idea reflection) are easily differentiated as well. For example, the literary and rhetorical analysis wheels automatically provide a framework for teachers to ask simple questions using only one element, or more complex questions by emphasizing relationships among various elements (e.g., how setting influences conflict, how figurative language contributes to characterization). Examples of simple and complex questions are included in selected lessons and also in Appendix A. Likewise, students who need more practice understanding a text may use the simpler text-based model (also in Appendix A) instead of the rhetorical analysis model. The teacher may also differentiate the in-class activities by assigning different groups of students to specific tasks. These can be designed as differentiated stations. Of course not all students would complete work at every station but would be assigned a station based on their readiness. After the complexity of the task is established, activities, questions, or product choices are then incorporated to accommodate various learning styles or interests.

The positive academic effects of grouping gifted students and accelerating the content they are taught are well documented (see the meta-analyses of Kulik & Kulik, 1992, and Rogers, 2007). However, not all middle schools are designed to support accelerated courses for their high-achieving students. Experienced teachers of general classrooms may use this unit with their gifted and high-achieving students as part of a deliberate differentiated approach that includes in-class flexible groupings and tiered questions, stations, and assignments.

ASSESSMENT AND GRADING

Formative, diagnostic-prescriptive, and summative performance-based assessments are an essential part of the unit. Assessment data come from a variety of sources and are used to monitor student growth, provide student feedback, allow for student self-reflection, or to differentiate content or instruction. Descriptions of the assessments used in this unit are as follows:

10

- **Diagnostic-prescriptive assessment:** The unit pretest provides a first glimpse of a student's current level of performance. Each question focuses on a different key understanding. For example, Question 1 focuses on the relationship between different literary elements, Question 2 focuses on making inferences and providing evidence, and Question 3 focuses on concepts or themes. Reponses for each question can be used to differentiate questions for different groups of students and to assign specific tasks that support student learning in a key area. Prior to Lesson 1, administer the pretest (p. 14) and use the rubric (p. 16) to score responses.

- **Formative assessment:** There are many opportunities throughout the unit for teachers to check for student understanding. Teachers may occasionally ask students to expand, in writing, upon their answer to an assigned question from the text-dependent questions of a particular lesson so that comprehension can be assessed. A rubric is provided as part of the Formative Assessment section in each lesson to check for understanding. This rubric can also be used to monitor student growth and to provide feedback. The ELA Practice Tasks and Formative Assessment sections may also be assigned and graded to determine the level of student understanding as well as misconceptions about specific sources or texts that may need reteaching or further exploration. It is not recommended that every lesson's formative assessment or ELA task be assigned or graded, although teachers may select two or three of each throughout the course of the unit to use for this purpose. Informally, teachers may gather formative assessment data by listening to student discussions to ensure that students understand the text. Differentiated choice products may also be used as a formative assessment and graded using the provided rubric. Teachers should encourage students to engage in self-reflection as they receive feedback from a variety of assessments.

- **Summative assessment:** There are two different summative assessments in the unit. The final lesson (Lesson 12) includes culminating choice-based products for students to showcase their understanding of key unit content, processes, and concepts through selected product-creations. In addition, the postassessment of the unit can also be used as a summative assessment and also to measure student growth, when compared with the preassessment.

EVIDENCE SUPPORT FOR THE UNIT

Besides the use of an evidence-supported Conceptual Framework (ICM), this unit was piloted in a variety of middle school classrooms with either cluster grouped or homogeneous groups of gifted students. Teaching training was provided and teacher feedback was solicited regarding lesson clarity, student engagement, and the impact on student achievement and engagement. Lessons were modified as a result of teacher feedback and student responses. Pre- and postachievement data were also collected for this unit.

Students who were exposed to at least five lessons (almost half the unit) showed significant growth as evidenced by their pre-post-performance on the provided assessments. The unit preassessment was administered to students prior to teaching and the postassessment was administered upon conclusion of the unit. Trained individuals who had no association with writing or teaching the units scored the assessments. Students ($N = 122$) made statistically significant pretest ($M = 1.24$, $SD = .382$) to posttest ($M = 2.04$, $SD = .463$) gains [$t(-16.345)$ $p = .000$] with important academic effects ($d = 1.48$) after correcting for dependence (see Morris & DeShon, 2002). This descriptive data suggest that after exposure to five or more lessons, students increase significantly in their ability to provide evidence or reasoning, justify a specific concept or idea, make inferences, and analyze specific literary elements.

Anecdotally, teachers reported that their students were more likely to notice connections among key ideas, concepts, literary and rhetorical elements, and multiple texts than before the unit was taught. In addition, their students discussed topics at a deeper level and offered more insights. They also liked that "teaching complexity was made easy" when using the unit's analysis models (e.g., literary analysis, rhetorical analysis) and as a result they were more confident that they were meeting the needs of their gifted learners than before unit implementation.

MAKING THE MOST OUT OF THE UNIT

The following ideas are important to consider before teaching the unit:

- Provide professional development about the units that includes both content and pedagogy. Some of the unit content is complex and background knowledge may be needed. Read Appendix A instructions and examples for using the analysis models before teaching the unit. Practice completing the models on your own using specific texts before asking the students to do so until you understand how the models are used.
- For those students who need more scaffolding, consider teaching the models separately first with easier texts to get students accustomed to different ways of thinking before adding complex resources, issues, and concepts.
- You may need to teach the individual elements of each analysis model before combining them. Still, it isn't necessary to teach an entire unit on mood or tone, for example, before using the literary analysis model, although stu-

dents may need explanations and practice applying the individual elements first if they haven't been exposed prior. Because gifted students learn at a faster pace, teaching individual elements can be done more quickly so that you can focus on depth and complexity through the relationships between the different elements. (This concept applies to each of the models.)

- Ensure that each individual lesson incorporates advanced content, an analysis model (e.g., literary, visual, or rhetorical), and links to the concept generalizations, as these are critical components of the ICM framework.
- Read the texts and prompts ahead of time to make sure the selections are appropriate for your district context. Substitute readings and visuals as appropriate. Make sure the online resources and YouTube videos are still available before teaching a particular lesson.
- Follow your students. Sometimes a lesson or reading may prompt important discussions that continue beyond the allotted time period.
- Know the intent of the models and the lesson outcomes so that you can best guide students toward important process, content, and concept goals. Otherwise, the issues discussed may supersede the objectives, especially with passionate gifted students.
- Consider informing parents of the unit contents and potentially controversial literature selections, concept discussions, and hot topics. Explain to them the main purpose and goals of the unit.
- Don't assign text-dependent questions as in-depth writing activities or homework as the norm. Discussion and teacher feedback are important and most of the questions in the unit are intended to be part of a small- or whole-group discussion. By engaging students through group discussions, you can correct misconceptions right away and solicit multiple perspectives and ideas that can enhance student learning.
- Be sure to emphasize the use of supporting evidence and the complex relationships among various elements of a model when facilitating student discussions.
- Have fun! We have enjoyed teaching these units and listening to teacher feedback. We hope these units not only show academic gains in your students but also encourage them to become citizens who can critically analyze situations and enact positive change.

UNIT GOALS AND OBJECTIVES

Content

Goal 1: To analyze and interpret literature, art, and media. Students will be able to:

- evaluate how literary or visual elements impact a work's overall message,
- explain with evidence how a writer supports a claim,
- respond to interpretations of texts through a variety of contexts by justifying ideas and providing new information,
- analyze how an individual's motivation and behavior are revealed, and
- relate interpretations of texts to the real world.

Process

Goal 2: To develop thinking, reasoning, and communication skills. Students will be able to:

- analyze meaning, purpose, and literary/visual elements;
- make inferences from provided evidence;
- reason through an issue (points of view, assumptions, implications);
- communicate to create, express, and interpret ideas; and
- analyze primary sources (purpose, assumptions, consequences).

Concept

Goal 3: To understand the concept of truth in the language arts. Students will be able to:

- make and defend generalizations about truth versus perception,
- explain the positives and negatives of knowing the truth,
- analyze the consequences of believing perception rather than truth, and
- explain the relationship between truth and other concepts.

Pretest

"Mercury and the Sculptor" *by Aesop*

Directions: Read the text and write your responses to the questions below, citing evidence from the text. After reading, complete the questions within 30 minutes.

Mercury once determined to learn in what esteem he was held among mortals. For this purpose he assumed the character of a man and visited in this disguise a Sculptor's studio. Having looked at various statues, he demanded the price of two figures of Jupiter and Juno. When the sum at which they were valued was named, he pointed to a figure of himself, saying to the Sculptor, "You will certainly want much more for this, as it is the statue of the messenger of the gods, and author of all your gain." The Sculptor replied, "Well, if you will buy these, I'll fling you that into the bargain."

Pretest, Continued
_____

QUESTIONS

1. How does the author's use of literary techniques (e.g., point of view, conflict, plot, language, symbolism, characterization, setting, etc.) contribute to the overall meaning of the passage?

2. "You will certainly want much for this, as it is the statue of the messenger of the gods . . . . " What inferences can be made about Mercury's motivation and conflict?

3. What does this story suggest about truth versus perception?

Name: _____   Date: _____

Pretest Rubric
"Mercury and the Sculptor" *by Aesop*

	0	1	2	3	4
Question 1: Content: Literary Analysis	Provides no response.	Response is limited and vague. There is no connection to how literary elements contribute to the meaning, main idea, or theme. A literary element is merely named.	Response is accurate with 1–2 literary techniques described with vague or no connection to a main idea or theme. Response includes limited or no evidence from text.	Response is appropriate and accurate describing at least two literary elements and a main idea or theme. Response is literal and includes some evidence from the text.	Response is insightful and well supported describing at least two literary elements and the theme. Response includes abstract connections and substantial evidence from the text.
Question 2: Inference From Evidence	Provides no response.	Response is limited, vague, and/or inaccurate. There is no justification for answers given.	Response is accurate, but lacks adequate explanation. Response includes some justification for either the character's motivation or conflict.	Response is accurate and makes sense. Response includes some justification about the character's motivation and conflict.	Response is accurate, insightful, interpretive, and well written. Response includes thoughtful justification about the character's motivation and conflict.
Question 3: Concept/ Theme	Provides no response.	Response is limited, vague, and/or inaccurate.	Response lacks adequate explanation. Response does not relate to or create a generalization about truth versus perception. Little or no evidence from the text.	Response is accurate and makes sense. Response relates to or creates an idea about truth versus perception with some relation to the text.	Response is accurate, insightful, and well written. Response relates to or creates a generalization about truth versus perception with evidence from the text.

Note: Adapted from *Jacob's Ladder Reading Comprehension Program: Level 4* (p. 148) by T. Stambaugh & J. VanTassel-Baska, 2001, Waco, TX: Prufrock Press. Copyright 2001 by Prufrock Press. Adapted with permission.

INTRODUCTION

Lesson

1

The Works of M. C. Escher

Goals/Objectives

Content: To analyze and interpret literature, art, and media, students will be able to:

- evaluate how literary or visual elements impact a work's overall message, and
- respond to interpretations of texts through a variety of contexts by justifying ideas and providing new information.

Process: To develop thinking, reasoning, and communication skills, students will be able to:

- analyze meaning, purpose, and literary/visual elements;
- make inferences from provided evidence; and
- communicate to create, express, and interpret ideas.

Concept: To understand the concept of truth in the language arts, students will be able to:

- make and defend generalizations about truth versus perception, and
- explain the relationship between truth and other concepts.

Accelerated CCSS ELA Standards

- SL.8.2
- SL.9-10.1
- SL.9-10.1c
- SL.9-10.1d
- W.9-10.4
- RI.9-10.7
- W.9-10.4
- W.9-10.5

Materials

- *Solo para Siempre* by Octavio Ocampo, available online
- *All Is Vanity* by Charles Allen Gillbert, available online
- *Relativity* by M. C. Escher (1953), available online

- *Still Life and Street* by M. C. Escher, available online
- YouTube video of Escherian Stairwells, available online
- Handout 1.1: Blank Visual Analysis Wheel
- Rubric 1: Product Rubric (Appendix C)

Introductory Activities

1. Explain that this unit will explore the concepts of truth and perception. Ask students to define truth. Discuss students' definitions.

2. **Engage students in a quick debate.** Challenge students to choose either agree or disagree (no in between) when presented with the following statements. Students can stand on opposite sides of the room to agree or disagree. Call on a few students to justify their answers from their own experiences. Challenge students to continue to think about these statements and their thoughts as they explore the unit. After the debate, ask them to define truth and perception.

    - It is best to know the truth.
    - Truth brings a person to freedom.
    - Truth is reality.
    - Ignorance is bliss.

3. Show students various optical illusions, such as *Solo para siempre* by Octavio Ocampo and *All Is Vanity* by Charles Allen Gillbert. Ask students to silently write what they see and then share their responses with a partner. Ask: *What makes these optical illusions interesting to you? Why do you think you saw one part of the picture before you saw another? Why do some people view one part of the illusion first and others see other parts first?* (Sample response: It depends on how one perceives the background, context, and contrast.) You may also want to show the blue-and-black dress perceived as gold and white, popularized in 2015 (search "dressgate" online). Ask: *Because much of the population sees it as gold and white, what does this reveal about the statement "truth is reality"?*

4. Introduce M. C. Escher (1898–1972). M. C. Escher is a famous 20th-century Dutch artist who is known for developing impossible structures within his art. He has made more than 448 lithographs and woodcarvings, and more than 2,000 drawings. Escher also wrote many poems and essays, and he studied architecture, although he never graduated from high school. He used many mathematical aspects in his works. Most of Escher's works involve his own fascination with the concept of reality. His works showing paradoxes, tessellations, and impossible objects have had influence on graphic art, psychology, philosophy, and logic. Show a few of his works to expose

students to his style, such as *Ascending and Descending, Metamorphosis I, Metamorphosis II, Metamorphosis III, Metamorphosis IV, Sky and Water I* (available online). Ask: *What ideas do you see in this art? What title would you give this?*

View Art

Display *Relativity* by M. C. Escher (without sharing its name). Conduct a whole-group discussion or Socratic seminar using the following questions:

- What behaviors do you see of the people? What do you notice about them?
- How many staircases are there? (Sample response: Six; some overlap.)
- How many sources of gravity are in this picture? (Sample response: Three.)
- What is the focal point of the picture? Justify your answer.
- How does Escher produce "dual effects" within this art? (Sample response: The ceiling is also a floor.) Although two people may be on the same staircase, they exist in two separate dimensions. Do the people know of each other's existence?
- Compare and contrast the people on the inside versus outside.
- Round robin: If you had to give the lithograph a title, what title would you give it? (Ask every student; short response.)
- Share with your neighbor why you chose this title. Tell students the real title of the lithograph: *Relativity*. Why do you think Escher gave it this title?

Note: Consider passing out copies of *Relativity* to each student. Students may color-code people existing on the same planes of reality (there are three planes of reality).

Visual Analysis

1. Distribute Handout 1.1: Blank Visual Analysis Wheel. Lead students through a basic understanding of each element, then emphasize the interaction of the elements with more complex questions (e.g., what techniques does the artist use to evoke emotion?). Note the inner wheel conceptually spins so that its elements interact with each other and the outer wheel. Refer to Appendix A for detailed instructions about the Visual Analysis Wheel. The Visual Analysis Wheel Guide (Appendix B) shows specific prompts to guide students in thinking through each separate concept. They may take notes on the Blank Visual Analysis Wheel (Handout 1.1) using arrows to show how concepts relate. See Appendix A for a detailed example visual analysis for this art.

2. The following questions and sample responses are a guide to elicit responses through scaffolding; however, multiple interpretations are encouraged as long as they are justified with evidence.

- **Purpose/Context:**
  - *What is the context of this art?* Lithograph printed in 1953.
  - *What do you think Escher's purpose/motive is in creating this?* To express an idea of reality; people perceive reality differently (students may not be able to determine this until after discussing the painting to some extent).

- **Point of View/Assumptions:**
  - *What is Escher's point of view toward reality?* Escher is revealing that there are multiple experiences and perceptions of reality.

- **Images/Technique/Structure:**
  - *What do you believe are the most prominent images in the picture? Why? How might they be symbols for something deeper?* Staircases = journey in life; featureless people = unaware, emotionless people; windows to outside = ways to get out of emotionless living.
  - *What techniques does Escher use to develop these images and enhance visual effects?* The people are all identical and featureless. There are three sources of gravity and six staircases. The outside world is park-like. Some appear to be climbing upside down, but according to their gravity, they are climbing the staircase normally. Parts of the picture look two-dimensional, other parts look three-dimensional. The people are engaged in casual acts (dining, going outside, climbing stairs). The basements add a surreal effect. *How does Escher intentionally place the objects in the painting to reveal meaning?* Help students see the two people standing on the same step—top center. They coexist yet they are in different gravity worlds. One is going up, one is going down, yet they are going in the same direction. *What does this reveal about life?*

- **Emotions/Technique/Structure:**
  - *What emotions does this evoke in you? What emotions are revealed? What techniques were used to evoke or portray emotion?* The featureless people reveal a lack of emotion, indicative that people are coming and going in life in an emotionless state. The lack of emotion interplays with a main idea that the people are not aware of each other's existence, particularly in the other gravity worlds.

- *How did the artist organize his art to portray or evoke emotion?* It is interesting that the staircase structure is an upside-down triangle. Perhaps this is to give a more chaotic feel to the picture. Those within the staircases are "lost" in a world of coming and going, living life unaware beyond their own self-centered worlds.

- **Artist Background/Technique/Structure:**
  - *What do you know about the artist's background? How is the artist influenced by the historical context of his time?*
  - *What techniques does Escher use that are unique to his style and organization of ideas?* Escher creates impossible realities within this work (three gravity worlds existing as one). He is known for creating paradoxes in his art.

- **Main Idea:**
  - *What is Escher conveying about life in this painting? What is Escher's main idea?* Reality is relative to perception; each person has his or her own view of reality and may be unaware of others' realities.

- **Implications:**
  - *What are the implications of this painting on you, the viewer?*

- **Evaluation:**
  - *Do you like this art? Would you hang it in your home? Was the artist successful in presenting his ideas? Justify your answers with evidence.*

In-Class Activities to Deepen Learning

1. Display Escher's *Still Life and Street* (available online). Ask: *Can this exist in reality? This painting is known as an impossible reality because it is two distinct realities that exist together, although their coexistence would be impossible in reality. They can only coexist in the artwork.* Ask students to discuss the two realities of the painting:
   - dollhouses and books set up on a table, and
   - buildings made as book structures with giant tobacco stands in the middle of the street.

2. Ask: *Which reality is real? Is it possible for them to coexist? Explain why what appears as reality is not always reality. Make connections between the print and real life.* (Sample response: As in real life, two perspectives of an issue exist simultaneously.)

3. Show students a YouTube video on Escherian Stairwells (there are several available). Ask: *Is it possible for this to exist in reality?* (*Note:* There is much debate online whether Escherian Stairwells are hoaxes or real.)

Concept Connections

Discuss connections to truth versus perception by asking the following questions:

- Would M. C. Escher agree that truth and reality are the same? Explain.
- What general statements can we make about truth, reality, and perception based on this art?

Choice-Based Differentiated Products

Students may choose one of the following independent products to complete (*Note*: Use Rubric 1: Product Rubric in Appendix C to assess student products):

- Create your own optical illusions, dual effects, or impossible realities to demonstrate your understanding of the conflict of appearance versus reality. You may wish to research more about optical illusion effects online. Write an explanation of how your drawing shows this effect.
- Conduct a visual analysis on another work of Escher using the Visual Analysis Wheel. Include a generalization about truth versus perception or appearance versus reality.
- Choose two of Escher's works to compare and contrast based on at least five of the following attributes (use of impossible realities, symmetry, two/three dimensions, portrayal of gravity, tessellations, images, ideas, theme). Use a Venn diagram or a chart to show your comparisons.
- Choose two of the following quotes by Escher. Explain what you believe Escher is conveying about reality in these quotes, and draw a picture to illustrate the two quotes you have chosen.
  - "Are you really sure that a floor can't also be a ceiling?"
  - "Only those who attempt the absurd will achieve the impossible. I think it's in my basement . . . let me go upstairs and check."
  - "We adore chaos because we love to produce order."
  - "So let us then try to climb the mountain, not by stepping on what is below us, but to pull us up at what is above us, for my part at the stars; amen."

Concept/Theme	
0	Provides no response.
1	Response is limited, vague, and/or inaccurate.
2	Response lacks adequate explanation. Response does not relate to or create a generalization about truth versus perception.
3	Response is accurate and makes sense. Response relates to or creates an idea about truth versus perception with some relation to the art.
4	Response is accurate, insightful, and well written. Response relates to or creates a generalization about truth versus perception with evidence from the art.

Figure 1.1. Scoring guidelines for Lesson 1 formative assessment.

ELA Practice Tasks

Assign one of the following tasks as a performance-based assessment for this lesson:

- How does perspective affect meaning? Examine two of Escher's works and write an essay that addresses this question. Be sure to support your viewpoint with sufficient evidence from the art.
- What is Escher's central idea in "Relativity" and how is it developed? Refer to specific evidence from the art to support your answer.

Formative Assessment

1. Ask students to respond to the following prompt in a single paragraph: *Choose a work we have discussed in this lesson. What does it reveal about the big idea of truth or perception?*
2. Use the scoring guidelines in Figure 1.1 to evaluate students' responses.

Name: _____   Date: _____

Handout 1.1
Blank Visual Analysis Wheel

Directions: Draw arrows across elements to show connections.

Art Piece: _____

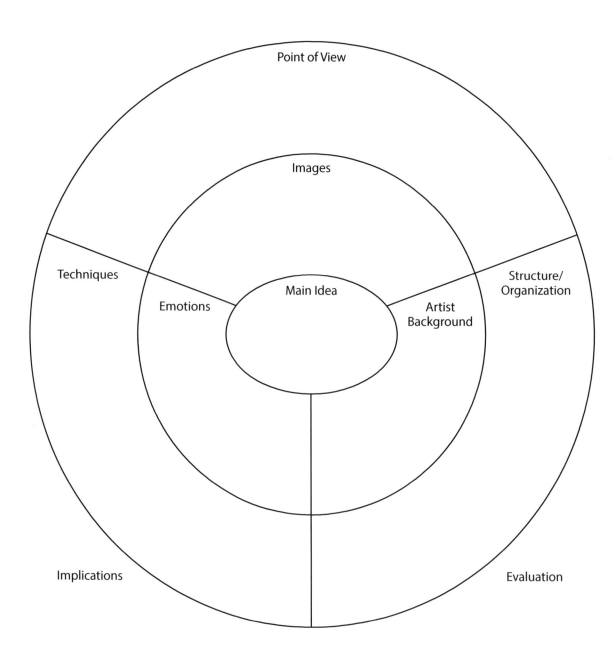

Purpose/Context

Point of View

Images

Techniques

Main Idea

Emotions

Structure/
Organization

Artist
Background

Implications

Evaluation

Created by Tamra Stambaugh, Ph.D., & Emily Mofield, Ed.D., 2015.

TRUTH:
An Examination of
What Is Perceived

Lesson

2

"Allegory of the Cave"
by Plato

Goals/Objectives

Content: To analyze and interpret texts and art, students will be able to:
- respond to interpretations of texts through a variety of contexts by justifying ideas and providing new information,
- analyze how an individual's motivation and behavior are revealed, and
- relate interpretations of texts to the real world.

Process: To develop thinking, writing, and communication skills, students will be able to:
- make inferences from provided evidence,
- reason through an issue (points of view, assumptions, implications), and
- communicate to create, express, and interpret ideas.

Concept: To understand the concept of truth in the language arts, students will be able to:
- make and defend generalizations about truth versus perception,
- explain the positives and negatives of knowing the truth,
- analyze the consequences of believing perception rather than truth, and
- explain the relationship between truth and other concepts.

Accelerated CCSS ELA Standards

- RL.9-10.1
- RL.9-10.2
- RL.9-10.6
- SL.9-10.1
- SL.9-10.1c
- SL.9-10.1d
- W.9-10.4
- W.9-10.5
- RI.9-10.2

Materials

- (Optional) Video: "Plato's Allegory of the Cave" (animated version; available on YouTube)

- (Optional) Calvin and Hobbes cartoon, "Did you ever wonder if the person in the puddle is real?", available at http://www.gocomics.com/calvinandhobbes/1988/04/26
- Handout 2.1: Excerpt From "Allegory of the Cave" by Plato
- Handout 2.2: Reasoning About a Situation or Event
- Handout 2.3: Concept Organizer
- Rubric 1: Product Rubric (Appendix C)

Introductory Activities

1. Ask: *Is there is a difference between reality and truth? If so, what is the difference?*
2. Ask: *What do you already know about Plato?* Fill in gaps for students. Plato was a Greek philosopher who influenced Western ideas. He was mentored by Socrates and he taught Aristotle. He published many dialogues between Socrates and others. Plato's work, *The Republic*, is a Socratic dialogue written in 380 B.C., which contains "Allegory of the Cave." In *The Republic*, Plato expresses ideas about a just society, the just man, and the just city. In the "Allegory of the Cave," Plato presents a fictional dialogue between Glaucon and Socrates. This allegory is ultimately about the role of education and a philosopher's place in society, to free prisoners.

Read Text

1. Distribute Handout 2.1: Excerpt From "Allegory of the Cave" by Plato. Have students read the text silently first. This is a difficult reading the first time through. Students may need to read the text two or three times for complete understanding.
2. After silent reading, ask students to draw a picture representing what they understand the cave to be like. Encourage students to ask questions for clarification and refer them back to the text to find clarification. Guide students by making sure that the drawings have the following:
   - Prisoners should be in chains looking at a wall with shadows.
   - Behind the prisoners should be a fire and various objects, which are reflected on the wall as shadows.
   - The picture should also include ascension to the outdoors (e.g., a staircase).

Note: Drawings of the cave can be found online for comparison.

Text-Dependent Questions

Select from the following questions for leading a Socratic seminar or class discussion:

- Describe the prisoners. (Sample response: They are in chains, facing the wall.)
- What do they see on the wall? (Sample response: Shadows of objects from behind them.)
- What do they view as truth? (Sample response: The shadows.)
- Why would a liberated prisoner experience distress? (Sample response: He is blinded by the light. Seeing the light can be just as blinding as being in darkness. His eyes have to adjust to the light to see the truth of what the shadows really are).
- Would the freed prisoner believe the real objects are real or illusions?
- What happens once the freed prisoner is out of the cave? (Sample response: He feels the need to go back to the chained prisoners to tell them the truth.)
- What might happen to the liberated prisoner when he returns to the cave? (Sample response: As stated by the text, he could be put to death because his "truth" is rejected by the chained prisoners who are content in their ignorance.)
- After reading the text, how would Plato define "reality"?
- According to the Allegory, how should we construct our knowledge of reality?
- Paraphrase: "The bewilderment of the eyes are of two kinds, and arise from two causes. Either from coming out of the light or from going into the light, which is true of the mind's eye, quite as much as of the bodily eye." (Sample response: One is blinded both in darkness and also by staring at the sun; likewise, one is hurt by living in ignorance [the darkness] but also in realizing the truth.)
- What do you think the shadows and light symbolize? (Sample response: Light is knowledge/truth; shadows are ignorance.) Ask students to justify their answers with evidence from the text.
- Write *disillusionment* on the board. Ask students if they know what it means. Break the word apart, noting the roots and affixes (not seeing the illusion, seeing reality). Disillusionment: Coming to know the truth, but it hurts (e.g, learning that Santa Claus is not real, realizing as you grow older that people in politics can be corrupt, etc.).
- How did the freed prisoner experience disillusionment? Cite examples from the text. (Sample response: He realized that he had lived in a cave all of his life that did not disclose the true realities.)

In-Class Activities to Deepen Learning

1. Show students a YouTube video on the "Allegory of the Cave" to further contribute to their understanding.

2. In small groups of four, ask students to reenact the "Allegory of the Cave." Students may consider adapting it to a present day skit. Students should be evaluated on portraying the basic plot elements: Prisoners believe the shadows are real, a prisoner escapes and is blinded by the sun, which hurts at first but then basks in the glorious truth of what the sun reveals, then this prisoner realizes reality and tries to go in and convinces the prisoners in the cave that the shadows are not reality. The freed prisoner risks death.

3. Ask students to create a Venn diagram comparing and contrasting the messages of truth/reality between Plato and Escher. (*Hint:* Escher's art conveys that perspective creates reality. Reality is relative to one's point of reference. Truth is perception. By contrast, Plato's message is that truth is reality, but people falsely believe that the perceived reality is truth. Truth exists regardless of perspective. Truth is absolute, those who do not see the truth are deceived. Both agree that what appears as reality is not always reality.)

4. Display a quote from Calvin and Hobbes (comic available online): "Did you ever wonder if the person in the puddle is real, and you're just a reflection of him?" How does this relate to what Escher and Plato have presented about reality?

5. Guide student through discussing "Is perception reality?" using Handout 2.2: Reasoning About a Situation or Event. Figure 2.1 provides some sample responses.
   - **Stakeholders:** Chained prisoners and freed prisoners (only two for this lesson).
   - **Point of View:** How the stakeholder(s) would answer the question, including evidence of why they feel this way.
   - **Assumptions:** Values and beliefs taken for granted by the stakeholders.
   - **Implications:** Short- and long-term consequences that happened or could have happened if that particular point of view were actualized.

6. Pose questions for small- or whole-group discussion:
   - How does Plato's Allegory relate to our world today? (Sample response: We believe in what the media portrays as reality; we believe propaganda we are presented; we tend to reject ideas that are unlike our own because we have never experienced those ideas ourselves.)
   - Who are chained prisoners and freed prisoners in our world? How do you know you experience truth or shadows? (Sample response: We have to critically analyze everything we are presented.)
   - What are the pros and cons of knowing the truth about our world? (Media, politics, government, etc., may be discussed.)

Stakeholders	Chained prisoners	Freed prisoner
Point of View	They believe they know the truth and view the shadows as reality.	He knows the true reality—the shadows are only reflections of reality.
Assumptions	They assume their reality is true since this is what they have experienced their entire lives.	He assumes he knows the true reality because he experienced the sun revealing the true realities. (Each group assumes they are right.)
Implications	They will reject the truth of the freed prisoner.	He takes a risk, but will try to share the real truth.

Figure 2.1. *Is perception reality?* Sample responses.

- What generalizations can you make about appearance versus reality conflict? How does this compare to what we said about Escher's work? (Sample response: Escher's views reveal that multiple truths exist; Plato's views reveal that one truth exists but the truth is perceived differently.)
- What is Plato's message about truth? (Sample response: When one finds truth, he is truly free; truth hurts; truth must be shared.)

Concept Connections

1. Guide students to understand how this allegory relates to the concept of truth versus perception. Explain that in this unit, they will focus on three major generalizations related to the concept/theme of truth and perception. They are:
   - Perception of truth varies.
   - There are negatives and positives in realizing truth.
   - There are consequences to believing perception rather than truth.

   Consider writing these on butcher paper or on the board for the duration of the entire unit. Throughout the unit, other generalizations can be added as students gain more insight into the concept of truth.

2. Use Handout 2.3: Concept Organizer to relate truth generalizations to the text. Students may work as pairs or individuals to complete their thoughts. Provide guidance as needed. Figure 2.2 provides possible responses; various interpretations are encouraged.

Perception of truth varies.
Shadows are mistaken for real objects.
There are negatives and positives in realizing truth.
The freed prisoner experiences pain when coming into the light until his eyes adjust to see the glorious beauty of realities. Then he wants to go back into the cave and share with others. Knowing the truth sets the prisoner free from his chains, yet when he re-enters, the prisoners want to kill him.
There are consequences to believing perception rather than the truth (truth being hidden).
The prisoners believe the shadows. They are content in ignorance.
Examine the relationship between truth, perception, power, ignorance, happiness, perspective, and/or freedom.
People are happy in ignorance. Those who know the truth have the power to share truth with others. Knowing the truth can be painful, but leads to freedom.

Figure 2.2. Sample student responses to truth versus perception generalizations.

Choice-Based Differentiated Products

Students may choose one of the following independent products to complete (*Note*: Use Rubric 1: Product Rubric in Appendix C to assess student products):

- Write a children's version of "Allegory of the Cave." You may want to create the same story through another type of allegory (e.g., allegory of the toy box). Include at least three illustrations. You may wish to change the setting and characters, but keep the message of how truth is perceived the same.
- Research more about Plato's concept of "Forms" in reality and present at least five facts and explanations to your classmates through a creative product of your choice (poster, brochure, handout, online poster developed from glogster.edu). Explain how the concept of forms is relevant in today's world and how Plato's theory of forms relates to "Allegory of the Cave" in an essay, pamphlet, or brochure.
- Create a dialogue between Plato and Escher, exchanging ideas about reality. Include a quote from "Allegory of the Cave" by Plato and at least one of Escher's humorous quotes, such as, "Are you really sure that a floor can't also be a ceiling? Or "Only those who attempt the absurd . . . will achieve the impossible. I think . . . I think it's in my basement . . . Let me go upstairs and check." You may wish to perform this in front of the class.

	Inference From Evidence
0	Provides no response.
1	Response is limited, vague, and/or inaccurate.
2	Response is accurate, but lacks adequate explanation. Response includes some justification for either the character's motivation or conflict.
3	Response is accurate and makes sense. Response includes some justification about the character's motivation and conflict.
4	Response is accurate, insightful, interpretive, and well written. Response includes thoughtful justification about the character's motivation and conflict.

Figure 2.3. Scoring guidelines for Lesson 2 formative assessment.

ELA Practice Tasks

Assign one of the following tasks as a performance-based assessment for this lesson:

1. Compare and contrast Plato and Escher's conceptions of reality. What generalizations can you make about both of them? How do they differ in their message about reality? Address these questions in a well-developed essay citing specific examples in your writing.

2. Is ignorance bliss? After reading Plato's Allegory, write a speech that addresses the question and analyzes the dilemma of hurtful knowledge versus ignorant happiness. Acknowledge both viewpoints, but develop an argument for your stance with sufficient evidence from the text.

Formative Assessment

1. Ask students to respond to the following prompt in a single paragraph: *What inferences can be made about the freed prisoner's motivation and conflict in the following text?*

   And if he is compelled to look straight at the light, will he not have a pain in his eyes which will make him turn away to take and take in the objects of vision which he can see, and which he will conceive to be in reality clearer than the things which are now being shown to him.

2. Use the scoring guidelines in Figure 2.3 to evaluate students' responses.

Handout 2.1
Excerpt From "Allegory of the Cave" *by Plato*

[**Socrates**] And now, I said, let me show in a figure how far our nature is enlightened or unenlightened:—Behold! human beings living in a underground cave, which has a mouth open towards the light and reaching all along the cave; here they have been from their childhood, and have their legs and necks chained so that they cannot move, and can only see before them, being prevented by the chains from turning round their heads. Above and behind them a fire is blazing at a distance, and between the fire and the prisoners there is a raised way; and you will see, if you look, a low wall built along the way, like the screen which marionette players have in front of them, over which they show the puppets.

[**Glaucon**] I see.

[**Socrates**] And do you see, I said, men passing along the wall carrying all sorts of vessels, and statues and figures of animals made of wood and stone and various materials, which appear over the wall? Some of them are talking, others silent.

[**Glaucon**] You have shown me a strange image, and they are strange prisoners.

[**Socrates**] Like ourselves, I replied; and they see only their own shadows, or the shadows of one another, which the fire throws on the opposite wall of the cave?

[**Glaucon**] True, he said; how could they see anything but the shadows if they were never allowed to move their heads?

[**Socrates**] And of the objects which are being carried in like manner they would only see the shadows?

[**Glaucon**] Yes, he said.

[**Socrates**] And if they were able to converse with one another, would they not suppose that they were naming what was actually before them?

[**Glaucon**] Very true.

[**Socrates**] And suppose further that the prison had an echo which came from the other side, would they not be sure to fancy when one of the passers-by spoke that the voice which they heard came from the passing shadow?

[**Glaucon**] No question, he replied.

[**Socrates**] To them, I said, the truth would be literally nothing but the shadows of the images.

[**Glaucon**] That is certain.

[**Socrates**] And now look again, and see what will naturally follow if the prisoners are released and disabused of their error. At first, when any of them is liberated and compelled suddenly to stand up and turn his neck round and walk and look towards the light, he will suffer sharp pains; the glare will distress him, and he will be unable to see the realities of which in his former state he had seen the shadows; and then conceive some one saying to him, that what he saw before was an illusion, but that now, when he is approaching nearer to being and his eye is turned towards more real existence, he has a clearer vision,—what will be his reply? And you may further imagine that his instructor is pointing to the objects as they pass and requiring him to name them,—will he not be perplexed? Will he not fancy that the shadows which he formerly saw are truer than the objects which are now shown to him?

[**Glaucon**] Far truer.

[**Socrates**] And if he is compelled to look straight at the light, will he not have a pain in his eyes which will make him turn away to take and take in the objects of vision which he can see, and which he will conceive to be in reality clearer than the things which are now being shown to him?

[**Glaucon**] True, he now.

[**Socrates**] And suppose once more, that he is reluctantly dragged up a steep and rugged ascent, and held fast until he 's forced into the presence of the sun himself, is he not likely to be pained and irritated? When he approaches the light his eyes will be dazzled, and he will not be able to see anything at all of what are now called realities.

[**Glaucon**] Not all in a moment, he said.

[**Socrates**] He will require to grow accustomed to the sight of the upper world. And first he will see the shadows best, next the reflections of men and other objects in the water, and then the objects themselves; then he will gaze upon the light of the moon and the stars and the spangled heaven; and he will see the sky and the stars by night better than the sun or the light of the sun by day?

[**Glaucon**] Certainly.

[**Socrates**] Last of he will be able to see the sun, and not mere reflections of him in the water, but he will see him in his own proper place, and not in another; and he will contemplate him as he is.

[**Glaucon**] Certainly.

[**Socrates**] He will then proceed to argue that this is he who gives the season and the years, and is the guardian of all that is in the visible world, and in a certain way the cause of all things which he and his fellows have been accustomed to behold?

[**Glaucon**] Clearly, he said, he would first see the sun and then reason about him.

[**Socrates**] And when he remembered his old habitation, and the wisdom of the cave and his fellow-prisoners, do you not suppose that he would felicitate himself on the change, and pity them?

[**Glaucon**] Certainly, he would.

[**Socrates**] And if they were in the habit of conferring honors among themselves on those who were quickest to observe the passing shadows and to remark which of them went before, and which followed after, and which were together; and who were therefore best able to draw conclusions as to the future, do you think that he would care for such honors and glories, or envy the possessors of them? Would he not say with Homer, Better to be the poor servant of a poor master, and to endure anything, rather than think as they do and live after their manner?

[**Glaucon**] Yes, he said, I think that he would rather suffer anything than entertain these false notions and live in this miserable manner.

[**Socrates**] Imagine once more, I said, such an one coming suddenly out of the sun to be replaced in his old situation; would he not be certain to have his eyes full of darkness?

[**Glaucon**] To be sure, he said.

[**Socrates**] And if there were a contest, and he had to compete in measuring the shadows with the prisoners who had never moved out of the cave, while his sight was still weak, and before his eyes had become steady (and the time which would be needed to acquire this new habit of sight might be very considerable) would he not be ridiculous? Men would say of him that up he went and down he came without his eyes; and that it was better not even to think of ascending; and if any one tried to loose another and lead him up to the light, let them only catch the offender, and they would put him to death.

[**Glaucon**] No question, he said.

[**Socrates**] This entire allegory, I said, you may now append, dear Glaucon, to the previous argument; the prison-house is the world of sight, the light of the fire is the sun, and you will not misapprehend me if you interpret the journey upwards to be the ascent of the soul into the intellectual world according to my poor belief, which, at your desire, I have expressed whether rightly or wrongly God knows. But, whether true or false, my opinion is that in the world of knowledge the idea of good appears last of all, and is seen only with an effort; and, when seen, is also inferred to be the universal author of all things beautiful and right, parent of light and of the lord of light in this visible world, and the immediate source of reason and truth in the intellectual; and that this is the power upon which he who would act rationally, either in public or private life must have his eye fixed.

[**Glaucon**] I agree, he said, as far as I am able to understand you.

[**Socrates**] Moreover, I said, you must not wonder that those who attain to this beatific vision are unwilling to descend to human affairs; for their souls are ever hastening into the upper world where they desire to dwell; which desire of theirs is very natural, if our allegory may be trusted.

[**Glaucon**] Yes, very natural.

[**Socrates**] And is there anything surprising in one who passes from divine contemplations to the evil state of man, misbehaving himself in a ridiculous manner; if, while his eyes are blinking and before he has become accustomed to the surrounding darkness, he is compelled to fight in courts of law, or in other places, about the images or the shadows of images

Handout 2.1, Continued

of justice, and is endeavoring to meet the conceptions of those who have never yet seen absolute justice?

[**Glaucon**] Anything but surprising, he replied.

[**Socrates**] Any one who has common sense will remember that the bewilderments of the eyes are of two kinds, and arise from two causes, either from coming out of the light or from going into the light, which is true of the mind's eye, quite as much as of the bodily eye; and he who remembers this when he sees any one whose vision is perplexed and weak, will not be too ready to laugh; he will first ask whether that soul of man has come out of the brighter light, and is unable to see because unaccustomed to the dark, or having turned from darkness to the day is dazzled by excess of light. And he will count the one happy in his condition and state of being, and he will pity the other; or, if he have a mind to laugh at the soul which comes from below into the light, there will be more reason in this than in the laugh which greets him who returns from above out of the light into the cave.

[**Glaucon**] That, he said, is a very just distinction.

[**Socrates**] But then, if I am right, certain professors of education must be wrong when they say that they can put a knowledge into the soul which was not there before, like sight into blind eyes.

Name: _____ Date: _____

Handout 2.2

Reasoning About a Situation or Event

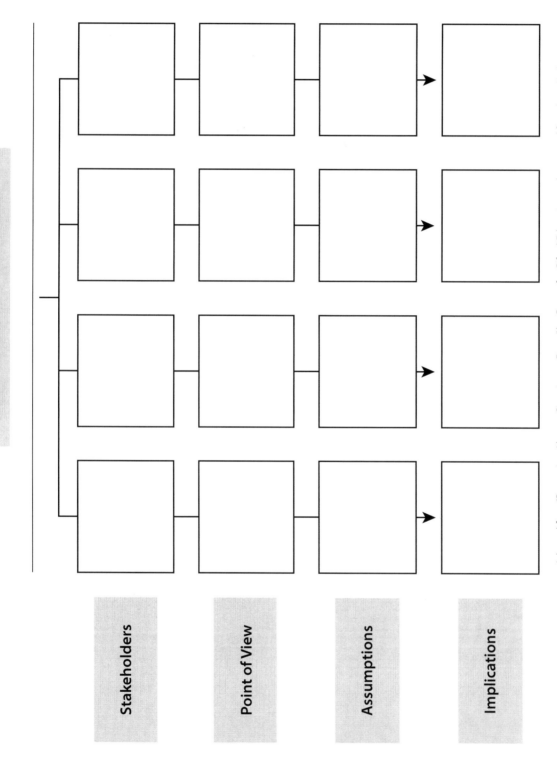

What Is the Situation?

Stakeholders

Point of View

Assumptions

Implications

Name: _____ Date: _____

Handout 2.3
Concept Organizer

Directions: How does each work exemplify each generalization? What new generalization can you make?

Literature, Art, or Media: _____	Literature, Art, or Media: _____	Literature, Art, or Media: _____
Perception of truth* varies. *(*"Truth" and "reality" can be interchanged to fit the context of the work.)*		
There are negatives and positives in realizing truth.		
There are consequences to believing perception rather than truth.		
Examine the relationship between truth, perception, power, ignorance, happiness, perspective, and/or freedom.		

Lesson

"The Lottery"
by Shirley Jackson

Goals/Objectives

Content: To analyze and interpret literature, art, and media, students will be able to:

- evaluate how literary or visual elements impact a work's overall message,
- respond to interpretations of texts through a variety of contexts by justifying ideas and providing new information,
- analyze how an individual's motivation and behavior are revealed, and
- relate interpretations of texts to the real world.

Process: To develop thinking, reasoning, and communication skills, students will be able to:

- analyze meaning, purpose, and literary/visual elements;
- make inferences from provided evidence; and
- communicate to create, express, and interpret ideas.

Concept: To understand the concept of truth in the language arts, students will be able to:

- make and defend generalizations about truth versus perception,
- explain the positives and negatives of knowing the truth,
- analyze the consequences of believing perception rather than truth, and
- explain the relationship between truth and other concepts.

Accelerated ELA CCSS Standards

- RL.9-10.1
- RL.9-10.2
- RL.9-10.3
- RL.9-10.4
- RL.9-10.5
- SL.9-10.1
- SL.9-10.1c
- SL.9-10.1d
- W.9-10.4
- W.9-10.5

Materials

- Student copies of "The Lottery" by Shirley Jackson, available at http://sites.middlebury.edu/individualandthesociety/files/2010/09/jackson_lottery.pdf
- Handout 2.3: Concept Organizer, continued from previous lessons
- Handout 3.1: Blank Literary Analysis Wheel
- Handout 3.2: Big Idea Reflection
- Rubric 1: Product Rubric (Appendix C)

Introductory Activities

1. Ask students to respond to the following question in a think-pair-share discussion: *What traditions does our American culture hold? Why do we have these traditions? What are the implications of these traditions on our society?*
2. Introduce vocabulary words that students will encounter in this lesson. Students may develop a chart for these vocabulary words (see Figure 3.1).
   - **Petulantly:** Showing sudden irritation due to impatience
   - **Perfunctory:** Carried out with a minimum of effort or reflection
   - **Exploitation:** The act of taking the greatest possible advantage
   - **Paraphernalia:** Equipment or items necessary for a specific activity
   - **Lapse:** A temporary failure of concentration, memory, or judgment

Read Text

Ask students to read "The Lottery" by Shirley Jackson. Consider conducting a scaled-down version of reader's theater. Students will read assigned parts of the story aloud. Although the story is not written as a play, it can still be read in parts if the students are savvy about following along and understand the dialogue.
- Narrator (change up every half page or so)
- Mrs. Hutchinson
- Mrs. Delacroix
- Various "people in the crowd" (small one liners of the villagers, the women, voices, Mr. Adams, Mrs. Adams)
- Mr. Summers
- Mrs. Dunbar
- Mrs. Graves

Text-Dependent Questions

Select from the following text-dependent questions for a Socratic seminar or class discussion:

Word	Know	Think I Know	Don't Know	Meaning
Petulantly			X	
Perfunctory				
Exploitation				
Paraphernalia				
Lapse				

Figure 3.1. Sample vocabulary chart.

- How would you characterize the mood in the first paragraph? What evidence supports this?
- What three words in the second paragraph best capture the scene described? How do you know?
- What can you infer about the roles of men and women in the village? Cite evidence to support your inferences. How do the women's "faded dresses and sweaters" relate to these roles? (Sample response: Women have less power than men.)
- How does the mood of the text change throughout the story? Cite specific words and phrases to support your response.
- Why is the discussion about other villages getting rid of the lottery important to the plot development? What does it suggest to the reader?
- Why is it important that the setting is on a warm, sunny day in June? Why is it important that a major character's name is Mr. Summers? (Sample response: The author hints that the lottery is positive just as the villagers are deceived into thinking that the lottery is a positive, necessary event for their society; likewise, readers are deceived at the beginning of the story in thinking that a normal event will happen. Mr. Summers's name seems cheery but in reality, he conducts a horrific event, highlighting a theme that evil can be disguised as good—appearance versus reality.)
- What is significant about the language patterns relating to "faded" dresses and "faded" black box? (Sample response: Their morality has faded.)
- What is significant about Mr. Summer's white shirt and jeans? (Sample response: It suggests that normal "good" people are capable of evil.)
- What is significant about the inclusion of children in the story? (Sample response: It shows that evil can be taught.)
- Which character cares most about fairness? (This should be debatable. At first students may say Ms. Hutchinson, but encourage other perspectives. She thought the lottery wasn't fair only after her family was chosen.)

- Does Jackson reveal any internal conflict among the characters? Why is this significant? (Sample response: No—the absence of internal conflict illuminates the lack of moral consciousness among the participants. Because the text is in third person objective, we know no thoughts of the characters—this is addressed later in the lesson).
- Is Ms. Hutchinson a hypocrite? Support your answer with textual evidence.
- Why did they conduct the lottery? Cite evidence. (Sample response: There is no real reason—it's pointless violence from tradition, which is Jackson's main point.)

After Reading Discussion

Guide discussion by asking the following questions:
- What are you feeling at the end of the story? Why?
- What did the author do to make you feel what you are feeling? (Sample response: The author does not allow the reader to know the thoughts of characters; the setting is sunny, warm; the event happens as an ordinary event, evil is disguised as good.)
- Why would a community have this kind of tradition? (Help students understand the concept of a scapegoat—they placed their guilt/sins onto one person and killed her; there really is no logical reason for this violence, which is Shirley Jackson's main point. Often there is pointless violence because we do not question the authority of "status quo" or "tradition" in our culture.)
- What literary devices does the author use to add suspense? (Lead this discussion by helping students understand the point of view, symbols, and foreshadowing in the remainder of this lesson.)

Literary Analysis

1. Introduce/review point of view (e.g., first person, third person limited, objective, and omniscient). Ask: *What point of view is "The Lottery" and why?* (Sample response: Third person objective—we do not know the thoughts of the characters; we only see the action.) *How would the story be different if it were written in a different point of view?* (Sample response: We would all know that the lottery was in fact about a stoning. The ending would not have been a shock to the reader. Third person objective gives suspense).
2. Introduce/review foreshadowing: a literary device in which the author provides hints or clues about what may happen later in the story. This can be created by mood, setting, symbols, and characterization. Help students understand that if they re-read the story, there are many hints and clues that

the lottery is in fact a horrific event. Ask students to work with a partner or individually. They should go back through the story and highlight symbols/evidence that foreshadow it as a horrific event. Additionally, they may note the times that the author makes it seem that the lottery is appealing (this is not foreshadowing, but a creative writing style to promote ambiguous feelings while reading). Have students develop a chart citing evidence of both uses of foreshadowing (see Figure 3.2).

3. Guide students through a literary analysis using Handout 3.1: Blank Literary Analysis Wheel. Lead students through a basic discussion of each literary element, then emphasize the interaction of the elements with more complex questions. Note the inner wheel conceptually spins so that its elements interact with each other and the outer wheel. Refer to Appendix A for detailed instructions about the Literary Analysis Wheel and how to make a hands-on model. Encourage students to cite textual evidence throughout discussion. The Literary Analysis Wheel Guide (Appendix B) shows specific concepts for each element of the wheel. They may take notes on the Blank Literary Analysis Wheel (Handout 3.1 and Appendix B) using arrows to show how elements relate. Consider making a poster of the Literary Analysis Wheel Guide to refer to throughout the unit. Focus on the following complex questions:

   ▪ How does the narrator's point of view influence the reader's response to the text? How does it influence the theme?
   ▪ How does the author's use of language help enhance the reader's understanding of setting? How does the setting influence the plot?
   ▪ How does Jackson's use of language show a shift in mood throughout the story?
   ▪ How does characterization contribute to conflicts within the text?
   ▪ How does an absence of internal conflict contribute to the theme?

The following notes may be helpful in guiding students through the analysis. Various interpretations are encouraged.

   ▪ **Themes:** Evil disguised as good, truth versus perception, following the crowd, following tradition/status quo, and the unexamined life.
   ▪ **Character:** Mrs. Hutchinson experiences the cruelty of her fellow villagers. She didn't ever question the tradition until her own family was called; therefore, she acted as a hypocrite and acted selfishly. She was only concerned with the inhumaneness of the event when it affected her personally.
   ▪ **Setting:** Because no specific place is mentioned, the setting is a blank slate so readers can project their own lives onto the story. The setting

Foreshadowing: Lottery is not desirable	Lottery is appealing: Author keeps the reader hopeful
"feeling of liberty sat *uneasily*"	Sunny, fresh, warmth of summer day
"stuffed his pockets full of stones"	Flowers were blossoming
Making piles of stones	Morning
Jokes were quiet, smiled instead of laughed	The lottery was conducted—as were the square dances, the teen club, the Halloween program
Children came reluctantly	Mr. Summers was a "jovial" man with a clean white shirt and blue jeans
Names of Mr. and Mrs. Graves, Mr. Warner	Name of Mr. Summers
Faded black box (stained)	"People separated good-humoredly"
Faded dresses and sweaters	Mr. Summers said "cheerfully"; waited with "polite interest"
There was "hesitation," blinked his eyes "nervously," "sudden hush," "wetting their lips," "gravely," repetition of "nervous" throughout, "long pause, a breathless pause"	Happened as an ordinary event in an ordinary village
Hutchinson repeatedly exclaims, "It's not fair . . . "	

Figure 3.2. Sample evidence of foreshadowing chart.

suggests that situations like this can happen anywhere if individuals neglect to live self-examined lives.

- **Mood:** Changes from warm ("sunny, warm"), to suspenseful ("nervously, hesitation"), to horrific. This allows the reader to be deceived into thinking that the story is about a good event, just as the citizens are deceived that what they are doing is actually good and necessary.

- **Conflict:** The absence of an internal conflict is due to the story being in third person objective. This also supports the idea that the villagers do not feel guilty for stoning a community member. The lack of moral consciousness illuminates the theme of an unexamined life.

- **Point of View:** Third person objective—we do not know what characters are thinking and feeling. We only know what they say. The reader is watching the story like a fly on the wall. This makes the story more suspenseful. If we knew what characters were thinking, the readers would know all along that the lottery is a stoning.

▪ **Language:** Names of characters—Graves, Warner, and Summers—importance of dialect of the women. The dialect of the characters also develops the setting.
▪ **Symbols:**
  • Mr. Warner: Foreshadow symbol for warning.
  • Mr. Graves: Foreshadow symbol for death.
  • Mr. Summers: Ironic symbol for normalcy and goodness (also his jeans and white shirt).
  • Black box: Tradition and loyalty, "black" = death.
  • "Faded dresses and sweaters": Women have less power than men.
  • The lottery: Ironic symbol—seems harmless to societies.
  • Stones: Ancient traditions of killing; everyone gets to participate in reinforcing the idea of group beliefs.
  • Delacroix: Translated as "of the cross" which paints the picture of how Jesus was used as a scapegoat; blame was put on him for the sins of the world. Other interpretation: Mrs. Delacroix "crucified" Tessie.
  • Boys gathering stones: Brainwashing of children participating in the horrific ritual.

Big Idea Reflection

Use Handout 3.2: Big Idea Reflection to help students transfer knowledge of the story to real-life.
  ▪ **Concepts:** Tradition, authority, collective blaming, evil, pointless violence.
  ▪ **Generalizations:** The wickedness of ordinary people can be just as cruel as criminals. There are negative consequences to blindly following tradition. Allowing evil to happen is evil. It's imperative to examine the reasons behind why we do what we do.
  ▪ **Issue/Problem:** To allow evil to happen or not; human rights versus tradition.
  ▪ **Insight:** We do not question evil until it affects us personally; we unquestionably follow authority and tradition.
  ▪ **World/Community/Individual:** Individual—do I do things without questioning the reason behind it? Community—bullying. People are not going to stand up against it unless it affects them personally. World—evil is often disguised as good. Though we know of human suffering in the world, many are reluctant to take a stand to help. The nature of human nature is often to act selfishly and guard your own.
  ▪ **Implications/Solutions:** To consider the importance of living an examined life—to question the "why" of our actions.

In-Class Activity to Deepen Learning

Discuss or have students respond in a journal (depending on level of scaffolding needed):

- How does the story relate to "Allegory of the Cave?" What keeps the villagers in ignorance? (Sample response: While the cave prisoners were blinded in ignorance, the villages are blinded by tradition. They see reality as the tradition [shadows in the cave], holding tradition in higher regard than individuals.)
- Who is the "freed prisoner" in this story? (Sample response: Throughout the story, the reader is deceived into thinking the lottery is a happy event, but is disillusioned to realize the horrific reality at the end of the story. The reader becomes the enlightened one. Students may believe Tessie is the freed prisoner, but all along she has known about the horrific reality, so it is arguable that she is truly enlightened.)
- How does the quote "Fiction reveals truth that reality obscures" by Jessamyn West relate to the story?

Concept Connections

Discuss connections to truth by asking the following questions. Students may reflect on concept connections using Handout 2.3: Concept Organizer, continued from previous lessons. Figure 3.3 provides some sample responses.

- How does the reader's experience relate to a truth versus perception generalization?
- What are the consequences to believing perception rather than truth?

Choice-Based Differentiated Products

Students may choose one of the following independent products to complete (*Note*: Use Rubric 1: Product Rubric in Appendix C to assess student products.):

- Think of times in history when defending the status quo ("we've always done it this way") has been used as a rationale to deny human rights (e.g., racial discrimination). Write a one-page essay to describe three ways history has defended the status quo and the consequences for defending the status quo. Use three primary sources in your research. Consider evidence, authorship, and motives for the primary documents in your study.
- Find a song with lyrics that go with a theme of the story. Describe how the lyrics of the song relate to a theme in "The Lottery" in at least three ways. Share the song with the class.

Perception of truth* varies. **(*"Truth" and "reality" can be interchanged to fit the context of the work.)**
The villagers are blinded by tradition. They perceive that it is appropriate to kill through the lens of tradition. The reader believes that the lottery may be a happy event due to the author's use of literary devices and euphemisms, when it is actually a violent event.
There are negatives and positives in realizing truth.
Ms. Hutchinson cannot accept the truth that her family member is chosen. Even in questioning this truth, she herself is "chosen" which leads to her demise.
There are consequences to believing perception **rather than the truth (truth being hidden).**
Violence continues because the villagers act through the lens of tradition rather than their appreciation for human life. They perceive that what they are doing is right.
Examine the relationship between truth, perception, power, **ignorance, happiness, perspective, and/or freedom.**
Perspective of truth is skewed by the power of tradition.

Figure 3.3. Sample student responses to truth versus perception generalizations.

- Rewrite the story in a different point of view. Keep the setting and the plot itself the same and do not rewrite the ending; change the story's effect, not the story itself. Your story should illuminate how the point of view affects the tone, development of conflicts, and characterization.

ELA Practice Tasks

Assign one of the following tasks as a performance-based assessment for this lesson:

- Compare the characters in "The Lottery" to the figures in Escher's "Relativity." What generalizations can be made about both works? Explain your answers in a well-developed paragraph, citing three textual examples.
- In an explanatory essay, explain how Jackson develops the theme, citing sufficient and relevant evidence from the text. Refer to literary elements such as setting, characterization, and conflict to support your explanation.

Formative Assessment

1. Ask students to respond to the following prompt in a single paragraph: *"Suddenly, Tessie Hutchinson shouted to Mr. Summers. 'You didn't give him*

	Inference From Evidence
0	Provides no response.
1	Response is limited, vague, and/or inaccurate.
2	Response is accurate, but lacks adequate explanation. Response includes some justification for either the character's motivation or conflict.
3	Response is accurate and makes sense. Response includes some justification about the character's motivation and conflict.
4	Response is accurate, insightful, interpretive, and well written. Response includes thoughtful justification about the character's motivation and conflict.

Figure 3.4. Scoring guidelines for Lesson 3 formative assessment.

time enough to take any paper he wanted. I saw you. It wasn't fair!'" What inferences can be made about Tessie's motivation and conflict?

2. Use the scoring guidelines in Figure 3.4 to evaluate students' assessments.

Looking Ahead

See Lesson 6: *Flowers for Algernon* by Daniel Keyes and Lesson 9: *Fahrenheit 451* by Ray Bradbury. You may choose to assign one of these novels now as independent reading so students are prepared to discuss the novels and perform key activities when the lessons are presented.

Name: _____ Date: _____

Handout 3.1

Blank Literary Analysis Wheel

Directions: Draw arrows across elements to show connections.

Text: _____

Purpose/Context

Setting

Mood

Language
Structure
Style

Symbols

Plot/
Conflict

Characters

Theme

Point of View

Tone

Interpretation

Created by Tamra Stambaugh, Ph.D., & Emily Mofield, Ed.D., 2015.

In the Mind's Eye © Prufrock Press Inc.
Permission is granted to photocopy or reproduce this page for single classroom use only.

Name: _____ Date: _____

Handout 3.2
Big Idea Reflection

What?	**Concepts:** What concepts/ideas are in the text?	
	Generalizations: What broad statement can you make about one or more of these concepts? Make it generalizable beyond the text.	
	Issue: What is the main issue, problem, or conflict?	
So What?	**Insight:** What insight on life is provided from this text?	
	World/Community/Individual: How does this text relate to you, your community, or your world? What question does the author want you to ask yourself?	
Now What?	**Implications:** How should you respond to the ideas in the text? What action should you take? What are the implications of the text? What can you do with this information?	

Created by Emily Mofield, Ed.D., & Tamra Stambaugh, Ph.D., 2015.

Lesson

Starry Night
by Vincent Van Gogh

Goals/Objectives

Content: To analyze and interpret literature, art, and media, students will be able to:
- evaluate how literary or visual elements impact a work's overall message, and
- respond to interpretations of texts through a variety of contexts by justifying ideas and providing new information,

Process: To develop thinking, reasoning, and communication skills, students will be able to:
- analyze meaning, purpose, and literary/visual elements;
- communicate to create, express, and interpret ideas; and
- analyze primary sources (purpose, assumptions, consequences).

Concept: To understand the concept of truth in the language arts, students will be able to:
- make and defend generalizations about truth versus perception,
- explain the positives and negatives of knowing the truth,
- analyze the consequences of believing perception rather than truth, and
- explain the relationship between truth and other concepts.

Accelerated CCSS ELA Standards

- SL.8.2
- SL.9-10.1
- SL.9-10.1d
- W.9-10.4
- W.9-10.5
- RI.9-10.7
- RH.9-10.1

Materials

- *Starry Night* by Vincent Van Gogh, available online

- Performance and lyrics to "Vincent" or "Starry, Starry Night" by Don McLean, as performed by Josh Groban or Chloe Agnew, available online
- Handout 4.1: Van Gogh: Fact or Fiction?
- Handout 4.2: Blank Visual Analysis Wheel

Note: This lesson illuminates Vincent Van Gogh's emotional intensities and suicide. Be sensitive in discussing the contents with students.

Introductory Activities

1. Ask: *What do you already know about Vincent Van Gogh?* You may wish to expose students to some of Van Gogh's paintings, such as *Sunflowers, Irises, Self-Portrait, Bedroom in Arles, Van Gogh's Chair, Starry Night Over the Rhone,* or *Starry Night.*
2. Distribute Handout 4.1: Van Gogh: Fact or Fiction? Then share information provided. Reinforce that it is okay for them to be wrong. This background knowledge will be important in interpreting *Starry Night.*
    - **Van Gogh was born in China in 1853.** Fiction. He was born in the Netherlands. He is a Dutch artist. The year 1853 is correct.
    - **Van Gogh's father was a minister in the Dutch Reformed Church.** Fact. Van Gogh also wanted to be a minister. While a missionary, Van Gogh slept in a straw hut as many of the poor people did in Belgium, and was said to be crying all throughout the night. He had a variety of jobs throughout his life including working for an art dealer, working as a teacher, being a minister's assistant, and working for a bookshop where he doodled and translated the Bible into English, French, and German.
    - **Van Gogh went to school to study theology to become a minister.** Fiction. He wanted to, however, he failed the entrance exam. He later went to art school and desired to become a great artist to serve God while painting. He stated ". . . to try to understand the real significance of what the great artists, the serious masters, tell us in their masterpieces, that leads to God; one man wrote or told it in a book; another in a picture." His main goal was to be a pastor of the Dutch Reformed Church.
    - **Van Gogh wrote more than 800 letters in his lifetime, mainly to his girlfriend and future wife.** Fiction. He wrote more than 800 letters, but most were to his brother, Theo. Most of these letters are preserved and can be read online.
    - **Van Gogh attended art school with Monet.** Fiction. He was a self-taught artist with little training. He probably met Monet and was inspired by Impressionism. Van Gogh, however, is considered a post-Impressionist artist.

- **Van Gogh shot himself in a wheat field.** Fact. He shot himself in a wheat field at the age of 37 and died 2 days later. Five months prior to this, he had admitted himself into St. Rémy's asylum.
- **Van Gogh painted *Starry Night* in an insane asylum.** Fact. It's a picture of his view from St. Rémy-de-Provence's asylum where he stayed for about a year—spring 1890–1891. He admitted himself as a patient.
- **Van Gogh sold more than 900 paintings during his lifetime.** Fiction. He painted more than 900 paintings, but sold only one, "The Red Vineyard." He only became famous after his death.
- **Van Gogh was psychologically unstable, causing him to cut off his entire ear in a fit of rage.** Fiction. In an epileptic seizure, he tried to attack his friend and artist Gauguin with a razor, and in this attempt, cut off part of his own ear, not the entire ear. He was then admitted to a hospital in Arles. He wrote, "Sometimes moods of indescribable anguish, sometimes moments when the veil of time and fatality of circumstances seemed to be torn apart for an instant." Five months later, he was admitted to St. Rémy.
- **Van Gogh was considered to have multiple psychological problems.** Fact. Current psychiatrists have suggested that his diagnoses range from schizophrenia, bipolar depressive disorder, and epilepsy. He suffered from many hallucinations and delusions.

Note: SparkNotes provides an excellent overview of Van Gogh's biography. Students may read it or teachers may consult it for more information: http://www.sparknotes.com/biography/vangogh/summary.html.

View Art

Conduct a whole group discussion on the painting. *Starry Night* is perhaps one of Van Gogh's most famous works. It was painted in 1889 while Van Gogh was looking out his window at St. Rémy's Asylum. Ask every student to respond in round robin (no discussion yet) to the following statements. This may be conducted as a Socratic seminar.

- What is the focal part of the painting to you (e.g., steeple, moon, lights in the city, etc.)? *Note:* Many students may not know what the black "bush" is. They may think it is a mountain or even a hairy monster. Most critics believe it is a cypress tree growing from outside his window of the asylum. This assumption is based on other paintings with this same image. You may not want to tell the students this, but guide them in figuring this out.
- What one word do you associate with this painting (e.g., moving, dark, loneliness, calm, peace, sadness, etc.)?
- Is this more about hope or despair? What evidence supports your response?

Visual Analysis

Use Handout 4.2: Blank Visual Analysis Wheel to discuss other elements of the painting. Lead students through a basic understanding of each element, then emphasize the interaction of the elements with more complex questions (e.g., what techniques does the artist use to evoke emotion?). Students can take notes on the wheel and draw arrows to illustrate connections between concepts. Use the following sample questions to the lead analysis. Multiple interpretations are encouraged.

- **Purpose/Context:**
  - *What is the context of this work?* Painted in 1889 at St. Rémy's asylum, one year before his suicide.
  - *What do you think his purpose/motive is in creating this?* Students may not grasp the purpose until the analysis is complete—to express his perspective of reality.

- **Point of View/Assumptions:**
  - *What is Van Gogh's point of view toward reality?* The heavens are more desirable than Earth.

- **Images/Technique/Structure:**
  - *What do you believe are the most prominent images in the picture? Why? Could they be symbols for something deeper?* Waves = movement of emotions; dark cypress tree = depression or feeling of isolation; steeple = reaching upward/faith.
  - *What techniques does Van Gogh use to enhance visual effects? What are your general observations?* Swirling stars = alive and hypnotizing effect; exaggeration of big stars = emphasis on the heavenly; dark lines dispersed throughout = adds depth; the sky and hills both look like the ocean = more movement; sky is brighter than the city = the heavens are more glorious/appealing than the earthly town. This is in contrast to reality where a city would be brighter than the night sky. Van Gogh uses perspective to bring the sky to the forefront of the painting. Also, perspective emphasizes the enormity of the dark cypress tree. The waves seem to move from right to left, giving the painting order instead of randomness.
  - *How does Van Gogh intentionally place the objects in the painting to reveal meaning?* Consider prominence of the sky over the landscape; prominence of the dark cypress tree as compared to the small church, blocking the view.

- **Emotions/Technique/Structure:**
  - *What emotions does this evoke in you? What emotions are revealed? What techniques were used to evoke or portray emotion?* The swirling motion and blues evokes a sense of calmness (also refer to discussion in main idea—hope versus despair).
  - *How did the artist organize his art to portray or evoke emotion?* The prominence of the dark cypress tree evokes despair; the brightness of the sky compared to the landscape shows a sense of longing for the heavens.

- **Artist Background/Technique/Structure:**
  - Remind students of information from fact/fiction activity.

- **Main Idea:**
  - *Is Van Gogh painting a message of hope or despair? Cite evidence to support your response.* Hope—elements reaching upward, the heavenly skies are brighter than the Earth and the stars/light are exaggerated. Despair—the isolated cypress tree is dark, the colors are sad; life—the painting is full of movement and the moon is depicted as bright as the sun. Help students understand there is a stark contrast between the possible themes. Perhaps the painting is showing his inner conflict between his hopefulness and despair. The ambiguity is perhaps one reason why the painting is so well loved. What is perceived by one person is different from another. The "truth" of his message can only be interpreted.

- **Implications:**
  - *This is one of the most famous paintings of all time. Why do you think this is so?*

- **Evaluation:**
  - *Do you like this art? Would you hang it in your home? Was the artist successful in presenting his ideas? Justify your answers with evidence.*

In-Class Activities to Deepen Learning

1. Have students respond to the following questions as a whole group, in small groups, or individually.
   - How does Van Gogh's perspective on life shape his understanding of reality?
   - Relate to previous lessons: Compare and contrast how Escher and Van Gogh's visual perspective influences perception of reality. (Sample

response: Van Gogh reveals ambiguity of emotions; Escher displays ambiguity of existence.)

- ▪ Relate visual perspective of artists to literary point of view of authors. How do they compare in influencing one's interpretation of the work? (Sample response: Visual techniques can influence one to have an emotional connection to the work, and one may see realities that can only exist in art. Literary point of view allows the reader to interpret the story only through the lens of a narrator—depending on the view of the narrator, different levels of emotional reactions occur.)

2. Show students an optical illusion with *Starry Night* from http://imgur.com/gallery/VIeMk. After staring at black and white swirls for 30 seconds, the image will appear to move. Ask: *What new insight does this give you about this painting?*

3. Play "Vincent," also named "Starry, Starry Night," written by Don McLean. The song is performed by Josh Groban and Chloe Agnew (available on iTunes or YouTube). Distribute copies of lyrics. Explain that parts of the song are referring to other paintings of his, including his self-portrait. Play the song once or twice with students following the lyrics and underlining phrases they particularly find appealing. Ask:

- ▪ What phrases do you especially like in this song?
- ▪ Does this song shed any new insight into the painting for you? If so, what?
- ▪ What do you think is meant by "how you suffered for your sanity?" Would it have been more obvious for the writer to write "how you suffered for insanity"? Why do you think the author did this? (Help students realize that the insanity is about perspective. The world did not appreciate his genius and his beauty until after his death. Who are the "crazy" ones? This is a matter of perspective.)
- ▪ How do you interpret "And how you tried to set them free, they did not listen, they did not know how?" How does this relate to perspective? (Sample response: Van Gogh was the one in the asylum, yet the songwriter puts "them" in captivity, again switching the perspective. Perhaps Van Gogh's perspective on reality is the more true, beautiful way of looking at things.)
- ▪ Throughout the song, the writer says, "they did not listen, they did not know how, perhaps they'll listen now" until the very end, these words change, "they're not listening still, perhaps they never will." Why do you think the songwriter did this? What are they not listening to? (Sample response: His interpretation of beauty in despair, his battle between madness and genius.)

- How does the line "And how you tried to set them free" relate to the "Allegory of the Cave?" (Sample response: Van Gogh can see and express reality in a beautiful, genius way, yet others could not appreciate it; likewise, the freed prisoner who saw the sun and reality was obliged to return to the prisoners, though he risked rejection.)

Concept Connections

Ask the following questions to help students relate content to concept generalizations. Figure 4.1 provides some sample responses.

- What does *Starry Night* reveal about Van Gogh's perception of reality?
- What perception does Van Gogh believe about reality and what are the consequences?
- The world did not perceive Van Gogh's genius during his lifetime. How does this relate to a generalization about truth versus perception?

Choice-Based Differentiated Products

Students may choose one of the following independent products to complete (*Note*: Use Rubric 1: Product Rubric in Appendix C to assess student products):

- Write a letter to Van Gogh asking him at least five questions that you would like to know about his life and paintings. Also, with respect to the lyrics "Now I understand what you tried to say to me" explain to him what you think he was trying to say to you in *Starry Night*. Students can learn more about Van Gogh's life by reading some of his letters he wrote to his brother (see http://vangoghletters.org/vg).
- Think of another song that matches the mood of the painting *Starry Night*. Explain why the song complements the painting with at least four supporting features of the music (e.g., lyrics, use of elements in music, etc.).
- Draw a picture conveying an emotional conflict. Apply at least three techniques Van Gogh used in *Starry Night* (exaggeration, perspective, movement, swirling, and broad strokes) in your own drawing or painting. Consider adapting *Starry Night* to a new setting or point of view.
- Apply the role of a historian and consult primary documents of letters from Van Gogh written to various friends (e.g., Theo, Gauguin, and others). Analyze at least five letters by considering the purpose of the letter, Van Gogh's assumptions, the meaning, and the possible consequences of the letters. How did content change over time? What new insight do these letters give regarding Van Gogh's life and art?

Perception of truth* varies.
(*"Truth" and "reality" can be interchanged to fit the context of the work.)
The painting shows his perception of reality—hopefulness amidst a dark night shown in the flaming flowers and cypress tree reaching upward (symbolizing hope). Van Gogh appeared to be a crazy man, but in reality he is a genius and appreciated today.
There are negatives and positives in realizing truth.
Van Gogh could not cope with his reality; hence being in St. Rémy's asylum. His ultimate way of not coping with reality was suicide.
There are consequences to believing perception rather than the truth (truth being hidden).
Van Gogh perceived a better life in the heavens. Soon after this painting, he killed himself, thinking that death would be better than his own reality.
Examine the relationship between truth, perception, power, ignorance, happiness, perspective, and/or freedom.
Perspective of reality shows Van Gogh's desire for freedom from pain to achieve personal happiness amidst a dark time in his own life.

Figure 4.1. Sample student responses to truth versus perception generalizations.

ELA Practice Tasks

Assign one of the following tasks as a performance-based assessment for this lesson:

- Contrast the ideas and emotions revealed in M. C. Escher's *Relativity* to Van Gogh's *Starry Night*. How do the artists' techniques contribute to the emotional reaction of the viewer? Explain your answer in a well-developed essay, citing at least three examples from the each work.
- Does Van Gogh reveal more hope or despair in *Starry Night*? In an argumentative essay, defend your claim with relevant evidence from the art.

Formative Assessment

1. Ask students to respond to the following prompt in a single paragraph: *How does Van Gogh's use of artistic techniques contribute to the big idea in the work* Starry Night? *Include at least three artistic techniques to support your answer.*
2. Use the scoring guidelines in Figure 4.2 to evaluate students' assessments.

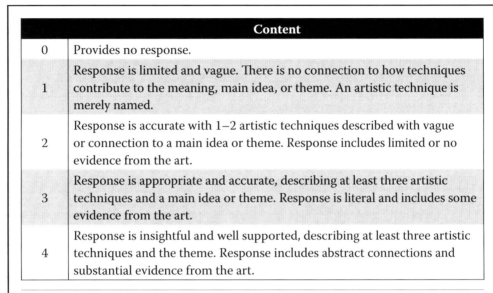

	Content
0	Provides no response.
1	Response is limited and vague. There is no connection to how techniques contribute to the meaning, main idea, or theme. An artistic technique is merely named.
2	Response is accurate with 1–2 artistic techniques described with vague or connection to a main idea or theme. Response includes limited or no evidence from the art.
3	Response is appropriate and accurate, describing at least three artistic techniques and a main idea or theme. Response is literal and includes some evidence from the art.
4	Response is insightful and well supported, describing at least three artistic techniques and the theme. Response includes abstract connections and substantial evidence from the art.

Figure 4.2. Scoring guidelines for Lesson 4 formative assessment.

Name: _____   Date: _____

Handout 4.1

Van Gogh: Fact or Fiction?

Directions: Determine whether you think each statement about Vincent Van Gogh is fact or fiction. Then, as you learn more information, take notes of important details about his life.

1. _____ Van Gogh was born in China in 1853.

2. _____ Van Gogh's father was a minister in the Dutch Reformed Church.

3. _____ Van Gogh went to school to study theology to become a minister.

4. _____ Van Gogh wrote more than 800 letters in his lifetime, mainly to his girlfriend and future wife.

5. _____ Van Gogh attended art school with Monet.

6. _____ Van Gogh shot himself in a wheat field.

7. _____ Van Gogh painted *Starry Night* in an insane asylum.

8. _____ Van Gogh sold more than 900 paintings during his lifetime.

9. _____ Van Gogh was psychologically unstable, causing him to cut off his entire ear in a fit of rage.

10. _____ Van Gogh was considered to have multiple psychological problems.

Name: _____ Date: _____

Handout 4.2

Blank Visual Analysis Wheel

Directions: Draw arrows across elements to show connections.

Art Piece: _____

Purpose/Context

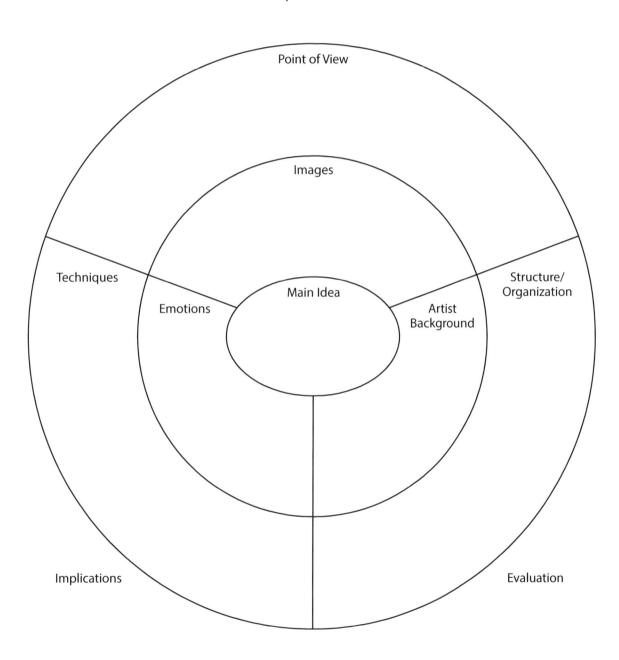

Created by Tamra Stambaugh, Ph.D., & Emily Mofield, Ed.D., 2015.

Lesson

5

Christopher Columbus's Encounter

Goals/Objectives

Content: To analyze and interpret literature, art, and media, students will be able to:

  - explain with evidence how a writer supports a claim,
  - respond to interpretations of texts through a variety of contexts by justifying ideas and providing new information,
  - analyze how an individual's motivation and behavior are revealed, and
  - relate interpretations of texts to the real world.

Process: To develop thinking, reasoning, and communication skills, students will be able to:

  - make inferences from provided evidence;
  - reason through an issue (points of view, assumptions, implications);
  - communicate to create, express, and interpret ideas; and
  - analyze primary sources (purpose, assumptions, consequences).

Concept: To understand the concept of truth in the language arts, students will be able to:

  - make and defend generalizations about truth versus perception,
  - explain the positives and negatives of knowing the truth,
  - analyze the consequences of believing perception rather than truth, and
  - explain the relationship between truth and other concepts.

Accelerated ELA CCSS Standards

  - SL.9-10.1
  - SL.9-10.1c
  - SL.9-10.1d
  - SL.9-10.4
  - W.9-10.4

  - W.9-10.5
  - RI.9-10.1
  - RI.9-10.2
  - RI.9-10.3
  - RI.9-10.4

  - RI.9-10.5
  - RI.9-10.6
  - RI.9-10.9
  - RH.9-10.1
  - RH.9-10.2

- RH.9-10.5
- RH.9-10.6
- RH.9-10.8
- RH.9-10.9

Materials

- (Optional) Student copies of "European Commercial and Financial Expansion," available at http://www.digitalhistory.uh.edu/disp_textbook.cfm?smtID=2&psid=3568
- Suggested reading for teachers:
  - "Hero Making," an excerpt from *Lies My Teacher Told Me* by James W. Loewen, available at http://www.thirdworldtraveler.com/History/Hero-making_LMTTM.html
  - "Discovering Columbus: Re-Reading the Past" by Bill Bigelow, available at http://urbanhabitat.org/node/960

- Handout 2.3: Concept Organizer (continued from previous lessons)
- Handout 5.1: Excerpts From Columbus's Log
- Handout 5.2: Blank Rhetorical Analysis Wheel
- Handout 5.3: Reasoning About a Situation or Event

Note: This lesson informs students of both positive and negative consequences of Columbus's encounter with the natives. Issues of the desire for Columbus to bring Christianity to the natives cannot be ignored, as they are written within the primary source text, but should be handled sensitively with students.

Introductory Activities

1. Go up to a student, take one of his or her personal items, and put it on your desk (e.g., a purse, a folder, a notebook). Say, *I found it, I'll take it!* Keep at your desk until the end of the lesson. This idea is adapted from Bigelow (1992).
2. Pose the following opening questions:
   - Why do we celebrate Columbus Day?
   - What are we celebrating?
   - Why do you think his contributions are acknowledged more so than other first explorers or even the American Indians? (*Note:* His encounter was the first that brought lasting communication between the Americas and the European world.)
   - What do you think would have happened if Columbus had not arrived in Hispaniola?

3. Help students understand the context of what was happening in 1492. Share with them the following facts as it will help them in understanding Columbus's log:

   - **January:** Moorish king of Granada (Muslim state on Iberian peninsula) surrenders to Ferdinand and Isabella, ending 10-year war.
   - **March:** Ferdinand and Isabella sign the Alhambra decree, declaring all Jews must leave the country unless they converted to Roman Catholicism. Clarify for students that Columbus sailed under the authority of Ferdinand and Isabella, the king and queen of Spain.

4. Ask students to read the article from Digital History about the background of Columbus. You may also ask students to do some initial research on the context of Columbus's exploration. Students need to develop an understanding that this event did not happen in a vacuum, but was a result of multiple historical events. You may divide the students into five groups to find and share at least five facts about the topics listed below. They may present a creative skit presentation about their assigned background knowledge.

   - Ferdinand and Isabella, conquest of Granada
   - Portugal's advancements in sea travel during the 1400s
   - Portugal's settlements off the West African Coast (especially the Canary Islands) and the influence on trading sugar cane and slaves
   - Columbus's early life and influences
   - The rise and fall of Taino (Arawak) Indians

Read Text

Distribute Handout 5.1: Excerpts from Columbus's Log. Explain to students that they will be analyzing a primary source document, Christopher Columbus's journal. They will be analyzing this document to understand Columbus's goals and purposes as well as the consequences of his actions.

Text-Dependent Questions

Select from the following questions to lead a class discussion or Socratic Seminar:

   - According to Columbus, who is his enemy? What do you infer about the historical, religious, and political context? What words and phrases make you think this?
   - According to the text, what is Columbus's purpose in going to India? (Sample response: To convert the Indians to Christianity.) As you continue

to read the text, describe how his purpose changes. (Sample response: He seems mainly concerned about finding gold.)

- According to the text, why is Columbus writing this? As you read the document, consider whether he accomplishes this purpose.
- What is Columbus's first impression of the natives?
- What is Columbus's cultural attitude toward the natives? Cite textual evidence. Why is this important?
- How does Columbus support his claim that the natives were "very poor people"? Would you agree with him based on what is described in the text (e.g., he also describes all the resources they have)?
- How does he support the claim that they would be easy to convert to Christianity? What evidence does he use?
- According to the text, how and why did Columbus's intentions toward the natives change from religious conversion to gold acquisition?
- How would you characterize the natives' attitude toward Columbus? Cite evidence.

Rhetorical Analysis

1. Briefly explain Aristotle's elements of rhetoric. Aristotle's rhetoric includes logos, ethos, and pathos appeals. These enhance a writer's ability to persuade an audience.
   - **Logos:** How the author establishes good reasoning to make the document/speech make sense. This includes major points, use of evidence, syllogisms, examples, evidence, facts, statistics, etc. Text-focused.
   - **Pathos:** How the author appeals to the audience's emotion. Audience-focused.
   - **Ethos:** How the author develops credibility and trust. Author-focused.

2. Use Handout 5.2: Blank Rhetorical Analysis Wheel to guide students through understanding how the main claim is established in Columbus's log. Students can examine how a writer achieves his or her purpose by analyzing how several factors work together to create an effective argument. Note the inner wheel conceptually spins so that its elements interact with the outer wheel. Refer to Appendix A for detailed instructions about the Rhetorical Analysis Wheel and how to make a hands-on model. The Rhetorical Analysis Wheel Guide (Appendix B) shows specific prompts to guide students in thinking through each separate element. They may take notes on the Blank Rhetorical Analysis Wheel (Handout 5.2) using arrows to show how elements relate. It is suggested that students first note the answers to each element separately on the graphic organizer, and then dis-

cuss the interactions. The following is a sample of questions and answers that could be used for the analysis.

- **Context/Purpose:**
  - *What is the historical context?* 1492—his first voyage. Europeans had newly developed skillful sailing practices using the caravel to travel the Atlantic. Portugal set up trading systems of slavery and sugar along West Africa. Columbus was familiar with these systems and saw opportunities for wealth when he arrived in the Caribbean. *Who is the audience?* The king and queen of Spain (Ferdinand and Isabella).
  - *What is Columbus's purpose in keeping the log?* To keep a log of events; to share information with the king and queen of Spain of his findings.

- **Claim:**
  - *What is Columbus's main claim?* Varies by different dates—natives will be easy to convert and dominate.

- **Point of View/Assumptions:**
  - *What is Columbus's point of view toward the Taino? What are his assumptions?* Columbus has the right to dominate and spread his own culture to them. He feels the natives are not strong and are easy to dominate.

- **Logos/Techniques/Structure:**
  - *What are Columbus's main points? How does the structure of the text help it make sense? How does he establish a rationale?* Columbus's logs are written in a chronological account (structure). He uses long sentence structure to develop his points. His main points are organized in the following way:
    - ◆ appeals to authority (king, queen, God),
    - ◆ descriptions of land and people, and
    - ◆ examples of why they will be easy to convert.

- **Pathos/Techniques:**
  - *How does Columbus develop emotional appeals?* Consider word choice in describing natives; he appeals to the king and queen's sense of pride.

▪ **Ethos/Structure/Techniques:**
- *Is Columbus credible and trustworthy? How and where does he establish credibility?* He refers to authority to establish his credibility, especially at the beginning. However, we must consider the extreme bias. Could he have stretched truth since he was writing to the king and queen?

▪ **Implications:**
- *What are the short- and long-term implications of this document?* Columbus is regarded as successful; he would be sent on more voyages for additional discoveries of riches. He inspired other future expeditions. He could have been regarded as a failure for not bringing back gold. The consequences are that Ferdinand and Isabella sent him on additional voyages, which resulted in the trading of "goods" (including people/slaves). The additional voyages would bring disease, which would kill large percentages of the Indian population. The natives were misnamed "Indians." Two worlds meet, which changes the world forever.

▪ **Evaluation:**
- *How effective is the author in supporting his or her claim?* Columbus's log is exceptionally biased from his point of view as he appeals to the pride and authority of Ferdinand and Isabella. He supports the claim that the Taino will be easy to dominate through several examples and observations, although these are biased cultural assumptions.

In-Class Activities to Deepen Learning

1. Assign the following brief research topics to groups of students. Ask students to find some basic information about their assigned topic and share their findings with the class. This information will help facilitate discussion in forthcoming lesson activities.
   - **Columbus:** Motivations for first, second, and third voyages.
   - **Taino (Arawak):** What actually happened to them as a result of Columbus's arrival.
   - **Ferdinand and Isabella (Spain, late 1400s):** Their motivation to send Columbus and their reaction to his findings.

2. Reflect on beginning of the lesson. Ask: *How did my taking away (students' name) item relate to this lesson?* Help students understand the connection between the language of "discovering" versus "stealing." Hypothetically,

because the teacher has a more superior culture, the teacher has the "right" to take what she wants. Help students understand that the teacher doesn't have a "better" culture, but a different one.

3. Help students understand the complexity of understanding Columbus within his own historical context. Consider reading the following aloud to students:

> The word "encounter" is now preferred to "discovery" when describing the contacts between the Old World and the New, and more attention has come to be paid to the fate of the Native American peoples and to the sensibilities of non-Christians. Enlightening discoveries have been made about the diseases that reached the New World through Columbus's agency as well as those his sailors took back with them to the Old. The pendulum may, however, now have swung too far. Columbus has been made a whipping boy for events far beyond his own reach or knowledge and a means to an agenda of condemnation that far outstrips his own guilt. Thus, too little attention has recently been paid to the historical circumstances that conditioned him. His obsessions with lineage and imperialism, his seemingly bizarre Christian beliefs, and his apparently brutal behavior come from a world remote from that of modern democratic ideas, it is true; but it was the world to which he belonged. (Flint, n.d.)

4. Distribute Handout 5.3: Reasoning About a Situation or Event. Guide students to evaluate multiple perspectives of the issue, "Should the U.S. celebrate Columbus Day?" Figure 5.1 shows possible student responses.
5. Guide students to think about the positive and negative consequences of Columbus's actions by having students develop a chart like Figure 5.2 on their own paper.

Concept Connections

Guide students to understand that language is a powerful part in perspective ("new" world only from the perspective of the Europeans, "discover" is a biased word for "seized"). Lead students through a discussion using Handout 2.3: Concept Organizer. Students should list examples of how the history of Columbus demonstrates these concept generalizations. Figure 5.3 provides some sample responses.

Stakeholders	Those who agree	Those who disagree
Point of View	Yes—Columbus established the first lasting connection between Europe and the Americas.	No—he was not really the first explorer to "discover" America. His actions led to negative consequences for the Taino.
Assumptions	Assumes Columbus is a hero who deserves recognition for his achievements.	Assumes the value of considering the oppression and violence experienced by the Taino. May assume other explorers such as Vespucci should be equally honored.
Implications	Acknowledges the profound impact of Columbus—America may not be what it is today.	Other ways to celebrate the meeting of two worlds can be explored.

Figure 5.1. *Should the U.S. celebrate Columbus Day?* Sample responses.

Positive	Negative
Opened doors for the Western world to come to the Americas.	Brought enormous growth to trans-Atlantic slave trade.
Brought Western Europe to the forefront of world control.	Later voyages brought virtual extinction to the natives due to disease.

Figure 5.2. Positive and negative consequences of Columbus's voyage sample chart.

Choice-Based Differentiated Products

Students may choose one of the following independent products to complete (*Note*: Use Rubric 1: Product Rubric in Appendix C to assess student products):

- Write five log entries from the perspective of the Taino Indians upon Columbus's arrival. Include at least five facts from your own background research within your account.
- Write a newspaper article for Columbus's return back to Spain for the Spanish and Portuguese citizens. How is Columbus perceived? Include at least five facts from the lesson within your article. Be sure to include a date and picture.
- Apply the discipline of a historian. Read another explorer's logs and conduct a complete Rhetorical Analysis Wheel on a selected excerpt. What new insight does this give you about the historical context?

Perception of truth* varies. (*"Truth" and "reality" can be interchanged to fit the context of the work.)
He falsely believed he was in India and renamed the culture of the Taino to "Indians," which has lasted for centuries.
There are negatives and positives in realizing truth.
In knowing the truth about American history, we can respect the past and all perspectives involved and acknowledge their places in America's story.
There are consequences to believing perception rather than the truth (truth being hidden).
Columbus's perception of the Taino resulted in negative implications for them, but positive ones for Spain.
Examine the relationship between truth, perception, power, ignorance, happiness, perspective, and/or freedom.
The Western world's perspective of Columbus has had great power of influence on American history.

Figure 5.3. Sample student responses to truth versus perception generalizations.

- Should we celebrate Columbus Day? If so, how? If not, how should the arrival of Western culture in the Americas be appropriately honored? Write a persuasive essay explaining your viewpoint using facts from this lesson to support your argument. Consider submitting the essay as an editorial to your local newspaper.

ELA Practice Tasks

Assign one of the following tasks as a performance-based assessment for this lesson:

- Consult three history textbooks. Evaluate how Columbus is portrayed in each text. Decide if the portrayal of Columbus is fair in each account. Defend your answer with knowledge from this lesson, citing evidence to support your claims. Develop your response in a formal report.
- What was the impact of Columbus's arrival on the Taino culture? After researching primary and secondary sources, write an article that explains the short- and long-term implications of the encounter. Use evidence from your research and cite sources appropriately.

	Concept/Theme
0	Provides no response.
1	Response is limited, vague, and/or inaccurate.
2	Response lacks adequate explanation. Response does not relate to or create a generalization about truth versus perception.
3	Response is accurate and makes sense. Response relates to or creates an idea about truth versus perception with some relation to the text.
4	Response is accurate, insightful, and well written. Response relates to or creates a generalization about truth versus perception with evidence from the text.

Figure 5.4. Scoring guidelines for Lesson 5 formative assessment.

Formative Assessment

1. Ask students to respond to the following prompt in a single paragraph: *Explain how various cultural perspectives regarding Columbus relate to the big idea of truth versus perception.*
2. Use the scoring guidelines in Figure 5.4 to evaluate students' assessments.

Handout 5.1
Excerpts From Columbus's Log

From *Journal of the First Voyage of Columbus*, 1492–1493

IN THE NAME OF OUR LORD JESUS CHRIST,

Whereas, Most Christian, High, Excellent, and Powerful Princes, King and Queen of Spain and of the Islands of the Sea, our Sovereigns, this present year 1492, after your Highnesses had terminated the war with the Moors reigning in Europe, the same having been brought to an end in the great city of Granada, where on the second day of January, this present year, I saw the royal banners of your Highnesses planted by force of arms upon the towers of the Alhambra, which is the fortress of that city, and saw the Moorish king come out at the gate of the city and kiss the hands of your Highnesses, and of the Prince my Sovereign; and in the present month, in consequence of the information which I had given your Highnesses respecting the countries of India and of a Prince, called Great Can, which in our language signifies King of Kings, how, at many times he, and his predecessors had sent to Rome soliciting instructors who might teach him our holy faith, and the holy Father had never granted his request, whereby great numbers of people were lost, believing in idolatry and doctrines of perdition. Your Highnesses, as Catholic Christians, and princes who love and promote the holy Christian faith, and are enemies of the doctrine of Mahomet, and of all idolatry and heresy, determined to send me, Christopher Columbus, to the above-mentioned countries of India, to see the said princes, people, and territories, and to learn their disposition and the proper method of converting them to our holy faith; and further-more directed that I should not proceed by land to the East, as is customary, but by a Westerly route, in which direction we have hitherto no certain evidence that any one has gone. So after having expelled the Jews from your dominions, your Highnesses, in the same month of January, ordered me to proceed with a sufficient armament to the said regions of India, and for that purpose granted me great favors, and ennobled me that thenceforth I might call myself Don, and be High Admiral of the Sea, and perpetual Viceroy and Governor in all the islands and continents which I might discover and acquire, or which may hereafter be discovered and acquired in the ocean; and that this dignity should be inherited by my eldest son, and thus descend from degree to degree forever. Hereupon I left the city of Granada, on Saturday, the twelfth day of May, 1492, and proceeded to Palos, a seaport, where I armed three vessels, very fit for such an enterprise, and having provided myself with abundance of stores and seamen, I set sail from the port, on Friday, the third of August, half an hour before sunrise, and steered for the Canary Islands of your Highnesses which are in the said ocean, thence to take my departure and proceed till I arrived at the Indies, and perform the embassy of your Highnesses to the Princes there, and discharge the orders given me. For this purpose I determined to keep an account of the voyage, and to write down punctually every thing we performed or saw from day to day, as will hereafter appear. Moreover, Sovereign Princes, besides describing every night the occurrences of the day, and every day

79

In the Mind's Eye © Prufrock Press Inc.

Permission is granted to photocopy or reproduce this page for single classroom use only.

those of the preceding night, I intend to draw up a nautical chart, which shall contain the several parts of the ocean and land in their proper situations; and also to compose a book to represent the whole by picture with latitudes and longitudes, on all which accounts it behooves me to abstain from my sleep, and make many trials in navigation, which things will demand much labor.

Friday, 3 August 1492. Set sail from the bar of Saltes at 8 o'clock, and proceeded with a strong breeze till sunset, sixty miles or fifteen leagues south, afterwards southwest and south by west, which is the direction of the Canaries.

Thursday, 11 October. Steered west-southwest; and encountered a heavier sea than they had met with before in the whole voyage. Saw pardelas and a green rush near the vessel. The crew of the Pinta saw a cane and a log; they also picked up a stick which appeared to have been carved with an iron tool, a piece of cane, a plant which grows on land, and a board. The crew of the Nina saw other signs of land, and a stalk loaded with rose berries. These signs encouraged them, and they all grew cheerful. Sailed this day till sunset, twenty-seven leagues.

After sunset steered their original course west and sailed twelve miles an hour till two hours after midnight, going ninety miles, which are twenty-two leagues and a half; and as the Pinta was the swiftest sailer, and kept ahead of the Admiral, she discovered land and made the signals which had been ordered. The land was first seen by a sailor called Rodrigo de Triana, although the Admiral at ten o'clock that evening standing on the quarter-deck saw a light, but so small a body that he could not affirm it to be land; calling to Pero Gutierrez, groom of the King's wardrobe, he told him he saw a light, and bid him look that way, which he did and saw it; he did the same to Rodrigo Sanchez of Segovia, whom the King and Queen had sent with the squadron as comptroller, but he was unable to see it from his situation. The Admiral again perceived it once or twice, appearing like the light of a wax candle moving up and down, which some thought an indication of land. But the Admiral held it for certain that land was near; for which reason, after they had said the Salve which the seamen are accustomed to repeat and chant after their fashion, the Admiral directed them to keep a strict watch upon the forecastle and look out diligently for land, and to him who should first discover it he promised a silken jacket, besides the reward which the King and Queen had offered, which was an annuity of ten thousand maravedis. At two o'clock in the morning the land was discovered, at two leagues' distance; they took in sail and remained under the square-sail lying to till day, which was Friday, when they found themselves near a small island, one of the Lucayos, called in the Indian language Guanahani. Presently they descried people, naked, and the Admiral landed in the boat, which was armed, along with Martin Alonzo Pinzon, and Vincent Yanez his brother, captain of the Nina. The Admiral bore the royal standard, and the two captains each a banner of the Green Cross, which all the ships had carried; this contained the initials of the names of the King and Queen each side of the cross, and a crown over each letter Arrived on shore, they saw trees very green many streams of water, and diverse sorts of fruits. The Admiral called upon the two Captains, and the rest of the crew who landed, as also to Rodrigo de Escovedo notary of the fleet, and Rodrigo Sanchez, of Segovia, to bear witness that he before all others took possession (as in fact he did) of that island for the King and Queen his sovereigns, making the requisite declarations, which are more at large set down here in writing. Numbers of the people of the island straightway collected together. Here follow the precise words of the Admiral: "As I saw that they were very friendly to us, and perceived that they could be much more easily converted to our holy faith by gentle means than by force, I presented them with some red caps, and strings of beads to wear upon the neck, and many other trifles of small value, wherewith they were much delighted, and became wonderfully attached to us. Afterwards they came swimming to the boats, bringing parrots, balls of cotton thread, javelins, and many other things which they exchanged for articles we gave them, such as glass beads, and hawk's bells; which trade was carried on with the utmost good will. But they seemed on the whole to me, to be a very poor people. They all go completely naked, even the women, though I saw but one girl. All whom I saw were young, not above thirty years of age, well made, with fine shapes and faces; their hair short, and coarse like that of a horse's tail, combed toward the forehead, except a small portion which they suffer to hang down behind, and never cut. Some paint themselves with black, which makes them appear like those of the Canaries, neither black nor white; others with white, others with red, and others with such colors as they can find. Some paint the face, and some the whole body; others only the eyes, and others the nose. Weapons they have none, nor are acquainted with them, for I showed them swords which they grasped by the blades, and cut themselves through ignorance. They have no iron, their javelins being without it, and nothing more than sticks, though some have fish-bones or other things at the ends. They are all of a good size and stature, and handsomely formed. I saw some with scars of wounds upon their bodies, and made signs to ask what they were; they answered me in the same way, that there came people from the other islands in the neighborhood who endeavored to make prisoners of them, and they defended themselves. I thought then, and still believe, that these were from the continent. It appears to me, that the people are ingenious, and would be good servants and I am of opinion that they would very readily become Christians, as they appear to have no religion. They very quickly learn such words as are spoken to them. If it please our Lord, I intend at my return to carry home six of them to your Highnesses, that they may learn our language. I saw no beasts in the island, nor any sort of animals except parrots." These are the words of the Admiral.

Saturday, 13 October. "At daybreak great multitudes of men came to the shore, all young and of fine shapes, very handsome; their hair not curled but straight and coarse like horse-hair, and all with foreheads and heads much broader than any people I had hitherto seen; their eyes were large and very beautiful; they were not black, but the color of the inhabitants of the Canaries, which is a very natural circumstance, they being in the same latitude with the island of Ferro in the Canaries. They were straight-limbed without exception, and not with prominent bellies but handsomely shaped. They came to the ship in canoes, made of a single trunk of a tree, wrought in a wonderful manner considering the country; some of them large enough to contain forty or forty-five men, others of different sizes down to those fitted to hold but a single person. They rowed with an oar like a baker's peel, and wonderfully swift. If they happen to upset, they all jump into the sea, and swim till they have righted their canoe and emptied it with the calabashes they carry with them. They came loaded with balls of cotton, parrots, javelins, and other things too numerous to mention; these they exchanged for whatever we chose to give them. I was very attentive to them, and strove to learn if they had any gold. Seeing some of them with little bits of this metal hanging at their noses, I gathered from them by signs that by going southward or steering round the island in that direction, there would be found a king who possessed large vessels of gold, and in great quantities. I endeavored to procure them to lead the way thither, but found they were unacquainted with the route. I determined to stay here till the evening of the next day, and then sail for the southwest; for according to what I could learn from them, there was land at the south as well as at the southwest and northwest and those from the northwest came many times and fought with them and proceeded on to the southwest in search of gold and precious stones. This is a large and level island, with trees extremely flourishing, and streams of water; there is a large lake in the middle of the island, but no mountains: the whole is completely covered with verdure and delightful to behold. The natives are an inoffensive people, and so desirous to possess any thing they saw with us, that they kept swimming off to the ships with whatever they could find, and readily bartered for any article we saw fit to give them in return, even such as broken platters and fragments of glass. I saw in this manner sixteen balls of cotton thread which weighed above twenty-five pounds, given for three Portuguese ceutis. This traffic I forbade, and suffered no one to take their cotton from them, unless I should order it to be procured for your Highnesses, if proper quantities could be met with. It grows in this island, but from my short stay here I could not satisfy myself fully concerning it; the gold, also, which they wear in their noses, is found here, but not to lose time, I am determined to proceed onward and ascertain whether I can reach Cipango. At night they all went on shore with their canoes.

Sunday, 14 October. In the morning, I ordered the boats to be got ready, and coasted along the island toward the north-northeast to examine that part of it, we having landed first at the eastern part. Presently we discovered two or three villages, and the people all came down to the shore, calling out to us, and giving thanks to God. Some brought us water, and others victuals: others seeing that I was not disposed to land, plunged into the sea and swam out to us, and we perceived that they interrogated us if we had come from heaven. An old man came on board my boat; the others, both men and women cried with loud voices—"Come and see the men who have come from heavens. Bring them victuals and drink." There came many of both sexes, every one bringing something, giving thanks to God, prostrating themselves on the earth, and lifting up their hands to heaven. They called out to us loudly to come to land, but I was apprehensive on account of a reef of rocks, which surrounds the whole island, although within there is depth of water and room sufficient for all the ships of Christendom, with a very narrow entrance. There are some shoals withinside, but the water is as smooth as a pond. It was to view these parts that I set out in the morning, for I wished to give a complete relation to your Highnesses, as also to find where a fort might be built. I discovered a tongue of land which appeared like an island though it was not, but might be cut through and made so in two days; it contained six houses. I do not, however, see the necessity of fortifying the place, as the people here are simple in war-like matters, as your Highnesses will see by those seven which I have ordered to be taken and carried to Spain in order to learn our language and return, unless your Highnesses should choose to have them all transported to Castile, or held captive in the island. I could conquer the whole

Handout 5.1, Continued

of them with fifty men, and govern them as I pleased. Near the islet I have mentioned were groves of trees, the most beautiful I have ever seen, with their foliage as verdant as we see in Castile in April and May. There were also many streams. After having taken a survey of these parts, I returned to the ship, and setting sail, discovered such a number of islands that I knew not which first to visit; the natives whom I had taken on board informed me by signs that there were so many of them that they could not be numbered; they repeated the names of more than a hundred. I determined to steer for the largest, which is about five leagues from San Salvador; the others were some at a greater, and some at a less distance from that island. They are all very level, without mountains, exceedingly fertile and populous, the inhabitants living at war with one another, although a simple race, and with delicate bodies.

Sunday, 16th of December. . . . your Highnesses may believe that this island (Hispaniola), and all the others, are as much yours as Castile. Here there is only wanting a settlement and the order to the people to do what is required. For I, with the force I have under me, which is not large, could march over all these islands without opposition. I have seen only three sailors land, without wishing to do harm, and a multitude of Indians fled before them. They have no arms, and are without warlike instincts; they all go naked, and are so timid that a thousand would not stand before three of our men. So that they are good to be ordered about, to work and sow, and do all that may be necessary, and to build towns, and they should be taught to go about clothed and to adopt our customs.

Name: _____   Date: _____

Handout 5.2
Blank Rhetorical Analysis Wheel

Directions: Draw arrows across elements to show connections.

Text: _____

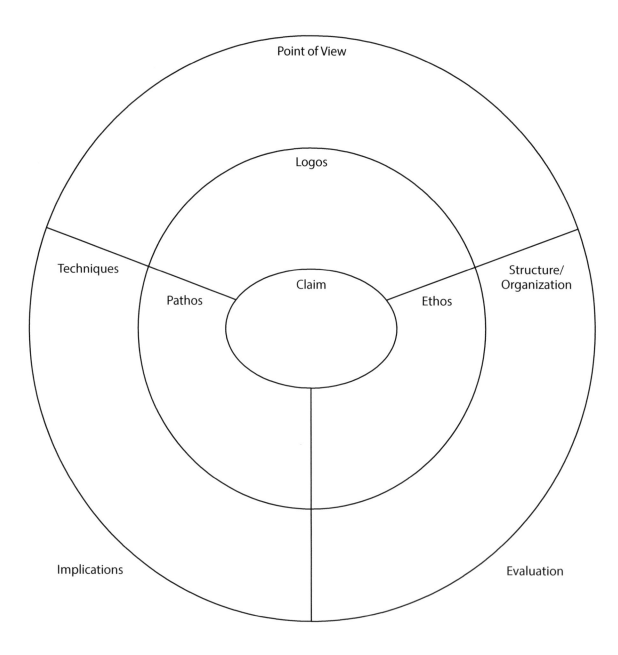

Created by Emily Mofield, Ed.D., & Tamra Stambaugh, Ph.D., 2015.

Name: _____ Date: _____

Handout 5.3

Reasoning About a Situation or Event

What Is the Situation?

Stakeholders

Point of View

Assumptions

Implications

Adapted from "Reasoning About a Situation or Event" by Center for Gifted Education, n.d., retrieved from http://education.wm.edu/centers/cfge/curriculum/teachingmodels. Copyright 2015 by William & Mary, Center for Gifted Education.

TRUTH:
An Examination of
Disillusionment

Lesson

6

Flowers for Algernon
by Daniel Keyes

Goals/Objectives

Content: To analyze and interpret literature, art, and media, students will be able to:

- evaluate how literary or visual elements impact a work's overall message,
- respond to interpretations of texts through a variety of contexts by justifying ideas and providing new information,
- analyze how an individual's motivation and behavior are revealed, and
- relate interpretations of texts to the real world.

Process: To develop thinking, reasoning, and communication skills, students will be able to:

- analyze meaning, purpose, and literary/visual elements;
- make inferences from provided evidence;
- reason through an issue (points of view, assumptions, implications); and
- communicate to create, express, and interpret ideas.

Concept: To understand the concept of truth in the language arts, students will be able to:

- make and defend generalizations about truth versus perception,
- explain the positives and negatives of knowing the truth,
- analyze the consequences of believing perception rather than truth, and
- explain the relationship between truth and other concepts.

Accelerated CCSS ELA Standards

- RL.9-10.1
- RL.9-10.2
- RL.9-10.3
- RL.9-10.4
- RL.9-10.5
- SL.9-10.1
- SL.9-10.1c
- SL.9-10.1d
- W.9-10.4
- W.9-10.5

Materials

- Student copies of *Flowers for Algernon* by Daniel Keyes. (*Note:* At teacher discretion, students may read the short story instead, available online.)
- (Optional) Outlines of Rorschach inkblots, available online
- (Optional) A one-page excerpt of *Canterbury Tales* (in Middle English), available online
- Butcher paper/markers
- Handout 2.3: Concept Organizer, continued from previous lessons
- Handout 6.1: *Flowers for Algernon* Reading Guide
- Handout 6.2: *Flowers for Algernon* Symbol Guide
- Rubric 1: Product Rubric (Appendix C)
- Rubric 2: Comparison Essay Rubric (Appendix C)
- Rubric 3: Collage Rubric (Appendix C)
- Rubric 4: Soundtrack Rubric (Appendix C)
- Teacher's Guide to Handout 6.2 (Appendix D)

Note: Parts of the novel include adult language and adult content (Charlie has an intimate encounter with Faye and Alice). It may be best to get parental permission before assigning the novel. You may wish to have students read the original short story instead. The short story does not have all of the literary symbols described in this lesson, but the themes are the same. The novel has several direct allusions to Plato's Allegory, while the short story has less. However, students will be able to see that Charlie's experience even in the short story relates to the released prisoner in Plato's Allegory.

This lesson focuses on student's independent reading of a novel/short story. You may assign the reading and activities to be completed independently while you continue to other lessons and revisit as needed to discuss, assign new activities, and check for understanding. Alternatively, you may choose to complete this lesson over the course of a week or two (depending on how quickly students read) before moving to Lesson 7.

Introductory Activities

1. Ask students to think about the cover of the novel. Depending on the publication, the kinds of questions will vary. Ask: *What could* Flowers for Algernon *mean? Who do you think Algernon is? What events are associated with flowers?*
2. **Engage students in a quick debate.** Ask students if they agree or disagree with the following statements. Call on students to discuss their reasons. (Optional: Ask students to respond to these prompts in writing.)

- It is better to be smart with no friends than to be mentally challenged with many friends.
- It is better to live in ignorance instead of knowing the hurtful truth.
- It is better to have loved and lost than to never know love at all.
- People with severe intellectual disabilities should be placed in an institution if their family does not want to help them.
- It is ethical to give someone surgery to make them smarter.

Encourage students to think about these statements throughout the unit.

In-Class Activities to Deepen Learning (During Reading)

1. Distribute Handout 6.1: *Flowers for Algernon* Reading Guide, which details activities for students to complete while reading the novel, and Handout 6.2: *Flowers for Algernon* Symbol Guide (a teacher's guide to this handout is provided; see Appendix D). Assign reading sections as you see appropriate for your students. You may wish to guide students through these activities at first, and as days progress, assign students to work in small groups on these activities. Depending on the pace of student reading, develop small groups/literary circles based on student progress. The following notes may be helpful as students complete the during-reading activities:
   - Examples of Charlie experiencing disillusionment:
     - **April 13:** Section regarding "Charlie, Charlie, fat head barley!"
     - **End of April 25:** Seeing Strauss and Nemur not as gods but as humans.
     - **End of May 8:** Realizing Gimpy is handling money unethically.
     - **End of May 15:** Professors are not giants.
     - **End of June 11:** Professors don't have all the answers.
     - **End of June 20:** Realizes that intelligence changed him.

   - Examples of allusions to Plato's "Allegory of the Cave":
     - **First page, before paragraph 1:** Excerpt from Plato's Allegory
     - **Paragraph before April 22:** "Like looking out of the kitchen window early when the morning light is still gray."
     - **April 27:** "Now I understand one of the most important reasons for going to college . . . to learn that the things you've believed in all your life aren't true, and that nothing is what it appears to be."
     - **Paragraph 11, May 11:** Reference to make-believe—"This kind of picture is a lie."

- **End of May 20:** "But what's wrong with the person wanting to be more intelligent . . . "—relates to prisoners rejecting the freed prisoner in the "Allegory of the Cave." "I'm like a man born blind."
- **May 25:** "I don't know. I'm like an animal who's been locked out of his nice, safe cage."
- **May 11:** Bright, dazzling night-lights of Times Square—"I'm confused . . . you're beginning to see and understand things . . . You're beginning to see what's behind the surface of things."
- **End of June 8:** Multiple references to "darkness" and "shadows."
- **Middle of June 11:** "They were just ordinary men, working blindly, pretending to be able to bring light into the darkness. Why is it that everyone lies? No one I know is what he appears to be."
- **June 24:** "I wanted to be with the people around me in the darkness."
- **August 11:** " . . . the work Charlie is doing is of utmost importance. His job now is to find the truth, wherever it leads." How does this have double meaning for Charlie? What is truth?
- **End of October 4:** "Plato's words mock me in the shadows on the ledge behind the flames; 'the men of the cave would say to him that up he went and down he came with his eyes.'"

- Examples of appearance versus reality:
  - **June 20:** "I eased myself into the chair. Incredible that he did not recognize me . . . . my appearance had changed even more in the past months. He studied me in the mirror." "I felt guilty at the deception."
  - **September 27:** "The most important thing had always been what other people thought—appearances before herself or her family."
  - Repeated references to the mirror.

2. Students can work in literature groups to discuss their journal responses, records of instances of the disillusionment and theme, list of symbols, and quote responses. Students should not simply read from their sheets but discuss their responses and ideas about these concepts. Students should ask each other questions, agree and disagree with each other, and be naturally interactive.

3. (Optional) If additional structure is needed, you may also wish to assign the following rotating roles, although you may want to be careful balancing the work load for students:
   - **Insights on Life:** Finds quotes that reveal specific insights/lessons on life.
   - **Realization Reader:** Finds realizations throughout the text of various characters.

■ **Conflict Counter:** Finds evidence of dilemmas encountered between and within characters.
■ **Question Maker:** Develops a list of five questions to ask various characters.

Content-Related Activities to Deepen Learning (During Reading)

1. Introduce students to projective tests (Rorschach tests, House-Tree-Person, free association). Some inkblots (or outlines of inkblots) can be found online. Show students various inkblots. Students should write down what they see. You may provide an interpretation (if available online). If interpretations are not available, students may develop their own theories about these responses. Help students understand how this relates to interpreting others' perceptions of reality and why these are not accurate assessments of personality.

2. Display a copy of a one-page excerpt from a Middle English version of *Canterbury Tales* (available online). Have students read the excerpt aloud to each other and summarize the content. Students most likely will experience difficulty just as a student with a learning disability can have difficulty. Ask: *What feelings did you experience in this activity? What insight does this give you about people who have learning disabilities?*

3. Explore the concept of emotional intelligence with students. Discuss: *How does emotional intelligence influence who a person is? Is someone's emotional intelligence always in line with his or her intellectual intelligence? What problems can this cause if they are unbalanced? As an advanced learner/ gifted student, have you ever experienced this?*

Concept Connections (During Reading)

About halfway to three-fourths through the novel, write the three truth versus perception generalizations each on separate pieces of butcher paper:
■ Perception of truth varies.
■ There are negatives and positives in realizing truth.
■ There are consequences to believing perception (appearances) rather than the truth.

Divide the class into three groups. Assign groups to a generalization. Students should write examples of how three characters experience the assigned generalization. Students should then share with the class.
Sample Response: Butcher Paper 1. Perception of truth varies.

- **Old Charlie:** The people at the bakery always made fun of him, he perceived it differently as new Charlie.
- **Alice:** Struggles with seeing the "real" Charlie (disguised by both ignorance and genius).
- **Professors:** Perceive that they are helping those with intellectual disabilities become more human, but the reality is that Charlie has been a real human being all along.

In-Class Activity to Deepen Learning (After Reading)

Using Reasoning About a Situation or Event (see Appendix B), have students consider the situation: "Was it worth it (e.g., was the pain and heartbreak worth the experience of knowledge?)?" Stakeholders include Charlie, Alice, and other characters of students' choosing.

Literary Analysis (After Reading)

Lead students through completing the Blank Literary Analysis Wheel (see Appendix B). Lead students through a basic discussion of each literary element, then emphasize the interaction of the elements with more complex questions. Encourage students to cite textual evidence throughout discussion. Students can take notes on the wheel and draw arrows to illustrate connections between concepts. The following notes are provided, but other interpretations are welcomed.

- **Context:** Written in 1966 (original short story published in 1958). Daniel Keyes was an English teacher and taught students with special needs. He was inspired to write this novel after a student with a learning disability asked him if he could be in a regular class if he worked hard to be smart enough. Keyes also had conflicts with his parents who did not approve of his career in English but wanted him to pursue medical school.
- **Purpose:** To entertain, to make audiences aware of the needs of people with intellectual disabilities, to explore the power of love.
- **Themes:** Appearance versus reality/truth versus perception, disillusionment, intelligence versus emotion.
- **Character:** Charlie learned to love Alice, to forgive, to deal with his past, to realize the truth about the professors (they are not intellectual giants), and that his "friends" were not really his friends when he was intellectually disabled. He learns that emotional connections are just as important as intelligence.
- **Conflict:** Charlie's main internal conflict is "Who am I?"
- **Symbols:** Tree of knowledge, window, mirror, Robinson Crusoe, Sta-brite, Algernon.

- **Point of View:** Mostly first person, which is Charlie's direct perspective, but as his perspective changes, the tone changes. Tone ranges from sincere naivety to jaded pessimism. The point of view changes to third person limited and omniscient in flashbacks. This supports the theme of disillusionment because Charlie expresses his disillusionment directly as the narrator.
- **Language:** Keyes' use of names—Norma, Rose; use of cave imagery—blindness, shadows, lights, darkness, cage, labyrinth, etc. to support themes and develop symbolism. (See Appendix D, p. 224.)

Big Idea Reflection (After Reading)

Use the Big Idea Reflection (see Appendix B) to help students transfer knowledge of the novel to real life.
- **Concepts:** Emotion, intelligence, disillusionment, disabilities, love, identity.
- **Generalizations:** It is better to know the hurtful truth than believe a comforting lie.
- **Insight:** Disillusionment is painful. The mentally ill deserve fair treatment. We all long for acceptance. Love is a powerful force. We are in need of self-examination of our past, present, and future. Intelligence is not enough, one needs love.
- **Problem:** Intelligence versus emotion, who am I?, etc.
- **World/Community/Individual:** Individual—What role does my own past play in the present and future? I'm growing up and realizing the harsh truths in life; Community—People will often make fun of people who are different. Everyone wants acceptance and love from friends.
- **Implications/Solutions:** In what ways might we address these issues?

Concept Connections (After Reading)

Discuss the truth versus perception concept generalizations. Students may reflect on concept connections using Handout 2.3: Concept Organizer, continued from previous lessons. Figure 6.1 provides some sample responses.

Choice-Based Differentiated Products

Students may choose one of the following independent products to complete (*Note*: Use Rubric 1: Product Rubric in Appendix C to assess student products unless otherwise instructed.):
- Write a comparison essay comparing Plato's "Allegory of the Cave" to *Flowers for Algernon*. Use at least three quotes from each work to support your arguments (see Rubric 2: Comparison Essay, Appendix C).

Perception of truth* varies. (*"Truth" and "reality" can be interchanged to fit the context of the work.)
The old Charlie believed he was loved and liked by his friends and family.
There are negatives and positives in realizing truth.
Charlie experiences disillusionment in understanding that he is smarter than his creators, his friends used to take advantage of him, and his family life was dysfunctional. This brings him emotional pain.
There are consequences to believing perception rather than the truth (truth being hidden).
After believing what was perceived for so many years as the old Charlie, the smart Charlie experiences emotional pain in his realizations of truth. He tries to find love and acceptance through Alice.
Examine the relationship between truth, perception, power, ignorance, happiness, perspective, and/or freedom.
The old Charlie believed he was loved and liked by his friends and family. Truth did not lead him to complete happiness.

Figure 6.1. Sample student responses to truth versus perception generalizations.

- Choose a theme in the novel. Create a collage (using a poster or virtual poster on a media site such as http://edu.glogster.com) to display elements of the theme. Include four supporting quotes from the novel, four additional quotes from other sources that relate to the theme, and eight pictures that are both abstract and direct representations of the theme. Include a written description of each element. Also consider the organization of your collage (see Rubric 3: Collage Rubric, Appendix C).

- What songs would you include on a soundtrack for this novel? Design a playlist of eight songs. For each song, write an explanation of why the song goes with a specific part of the novel. Develop a creative title and cover for your album. Be sure you include the specific relevant lyrics and specific parts of the story in your explanation. Share one song with the class (See Rubric 4: Soundtrack Rubric, Appendix C).

- Make your own set of five inkblots. Ask 30–50 people to say what they see. Record their responses. Try to categorize their responses and present the results on a graph (bar, line, or pie graph). Present your results to the class. Research how psychologists interpret a projective test (Rorschach, House-Tree-Person, incomplete sentences, or free association). Explain this in a brief one-page report in your own words. Include a list of your sources (at least four, including primary and secondary sources).

■ Research a brain disorder such as Parkinson's disease, Alzheimer's disease, aphasia, dyslexia, traumatic brain injury, or another disability or disorder of your choice. As you research the disorder, consider the research that has been done and research that needs to be done for the advancement of treatments. Develop an action plan to help address building awareness, raising funds, or promoting inclusion of these individuals within society. Teach the class about the disorder. Include a visual in your 10-minute presentation. Include a list of your sources (at least four). Include an activity in your presentation to engage the audience.

ELA Practice Tasks

Assign one of the following tasks as a performance-based assessment for this lesson:

■ In a well-developed essay, describe how the point of view changes over time in the novel. How does this affect the overall meaning of the text? Cite at least three specific examples to support your answer.

■ In a multiparagraph essay, compare Charlie to one of the prisoners in Plato's Allegory. How is reality perceived similarly? Relate their experiences citing specific examples from the texts to support your response.

■ Identify one of the themes in *Flowers for Algernon*. Write an essay in which you analyze in detail how the theme is developed in the text, citing sufficient textual evidence of the author's use of literary elements.

Formative Assessment

1. Ask students to respond to the following prompt in a single paragraph: *"I eased myself into the chair. Incredible that he did not recognize me . . . my appearance had changed even more in the past months. He studied me in the mirror . . . . I felt guilty at the deception."* What inferences can be made about Charlie's conflict and motivation?

2. Use the scoring guidelines in Figure 6.2 to evaluate students' assessments.

Inference From Evidence	
0	Provides no response.
1	Response is limited, vague, and/or inaccurate.
2	Response is accurate, but lacks adequate explanation. Response includes some justification for either the character's motivation or conflict.
3	Response is accurate and makes sense. Response includes some justification about the character's motivation and conflict.
4	Response is accurate, insightful, interpretive, and well written. Response includes thoughtful justification about the character's motivation and conflict.

Figure 6.2. Scoring guidelines for Lesson 6 formative assessment.

Handout 6.1

Flowers for Algernon Reading Guide

1. Maintain a recording log as Charlie does. Write from the perspective of Charlie, Alice, Dr. Strauss, or Dr. Nemur. Include at least 10 half-page entries from one of their perspectives. Date the entries and show the growth, realizations, and emotions of the character throughout.

2. Respond to the following questions in journal entries:
   - **Progress Reports 1–7:** Is it ethical for Charlie to have the surgery? Explain with three supporting arguments.
   - **Progress Report 16:** How do you think society should handle the placement of people with severe intellectual disabilities?
   - **Progress Report 17:** Why was it important for Charlie to learn about his past?

3. Keep a record of at least four instances in which Charlie experiences disillusionment. List the page number and summarize the experience.

4. Keep a record of theme references to appearance versus reality, cave, shadows, and light (relevant to Plato's Allegory). Cite specific quotes and explain their significance in their relationship to the theme of appearance versus reality. Specifically, what is Charlie learning and how is this similar to the freed prisoner? For example, in the paragraph before April 22, "Like looking out of the kitchen window early when the morning light is still gray" relates to Plato's cave because it is Charlie slowing stepping into light, out of the cave of ignorance.

5. Complete the following chart to explain the significance of each quote.

Quote	Insight on Life
March 8: "I just want to be smart like other pepul so I can have lots of friends who like me."	Sample response: *People long for acceptance.*
April 13: "People think its funny when a dumb person can't do things the same way they can."	

Handout 6.1, Continued

Quote	Insight on Life
April 14: "The more intelligent you become the more problems you'll have."	
May 15: "People resent being shown that they don't approach the complexities of the problem—they don't know what exists beyond the surface ripples."	
June 10: "Nemur's constant references to having made me what I am or that someday there will be others like me who will become real human beings."	
June 24: "I knew it wasn't the movies I wanted but the audiences. I wanted to be with the people around me in the darkness."	
July 20: "The meaning of my total existence involves knowing the possibilities of my future as well as my past, where I'm going as well as where I've been."	
August 11: "Intelligence and education that hasn't been tempered by human affection isn't worth [it]."	

In the Mind's Eye © Prufrock Press Inc.

Name: _____ Date: _____

6. Refer to Handout 6.2: Symbol Guide: *Flowers for Algernon*. Indicate the meaning of each symbol and if the symbol is also used to demonstrate foreshadowing, irony, or if it is an allusion. You may go back and determine if the symbols were foreshadowing devices, but this may come after reading.

7. Use the following table to describe how each of the characters experience the concepts of truth and perception.

	Perception of truth varies.	There are negatives and positives in realizing truth.	There are consequences to believing perception (appearances) rather than the truth.
Character 1: _____			
Character 2: _____			
Character 3: _____			

Name: _____ Date: _____

Handout 6.2
Flowers for Algernon Symbol Guide

Directions: Indicate the meaning of each symbol. Also determine if the symbol has other literary significance (foreshadowing, irony, allusion, characterization, etc.). If the symbol is referenced later, indicate the instance.

Symbol	Meaning	Other Literary Significance	Later Reference(s)
Adam and Eve, tree of knowledge, apple (March 12)	Apple = knowledge. Eating from the tree of knowledge was a result of *deception* from the serpent. Eating the tree opened their eyes to their nakedness—disillusionment.	Allusion: Reference to garden of Eden in Genesis.	*Paradise Lost* (Oct. 5).
Robinson Crusoe (March 30)			
Wax fruit (second April entry)			
Sta-brite metal polish (April 21)			
Three blind mice; carving knife (May 3)			
Picasso's *Mother and Child* (May 25)			
Courtier, masked, sword, protecting			

Handout 6.2, Continued

Symbol	Meaning	Other Literary Significance	Later Reference(s)
Norma			
Rose			
IQ of 185 and 70, distance (End of June 6)			
Window (June 10)			
Behavior of Algernon throughout the novel			
"Algernon was glaring . . . reflection in the mirror." (Toward the end of June 13)			
Maze/labyrinth			
Flowers for Algernon (title)			
Other Symbols			

Lesson

"The Necklace"
by Guy de Maupassant

Goals/Objectives

Content: To analyze and interpret literature, art, and media, students will be able to:

- evaluate how literary or visual elements impact a work's overall message,
- respond to interpretations of texts through a variety of contexts by justifying ideas and providing new information,
- analyze how an individual's motivation and behavior are revealed, and
- relate interpretations of texts to the real world.

Process: To develop thinking, reasoning, and communication skills, students will be able to:

- analyze meaning, purpose, and literary/visual elements;
- make inferences from provided evidence; and
- communicate to create, express, and interpret ideas.

Concept: To understand the concept of truth in the language arts, students will be able to:

- make and defend generalizations about truth versus perception,
- explain the positives and negatives of knowing the truth,
- analyze the consequences of believing perception rather than truth, and
- explain the relationship between truth and other concepts.

Accelerated CCSS ELA Standards

- RL.9-10.1
- RL.9-10.2
- RL.9-10.3
- RL.9-10.4
- RL.9-10.5
- SL.9-10.1
- SL.9-10.1c
- SL.9-10.1d
- W.9-10.4
- W.9-10.5

Materials

■ Student copies of "The Necklace" by Guy de Maupassant, available at http://www.eastoftheweb.com/short-stories/UBooks/Neck.shtml
■ Handout 2.3: Concept Organizer (continued from previous lessons)
■ Handout 7.1: Blank Literary Analysis Wheel
■ Handout 7.2: Big Idea Reflection
■ Rubric 1: Product Rubric (Appendix C)

Note: Consider consulting literary review sources such as http://www.sparknotes.com or http://www.cummingsstudyguides.net for further reading on the literary analysis of "The Necklace."

Introductory Activities

1. Wear a diamond necklace (can be fake) on the day you teach this lesson. Ask students: *Do you think this necklace is real? How do you know? Because you perceive it to be real, isn't perception of reality as good as the reality itself? What difference does it make to know that it is real or fake? What if you never know the truth of whether it is real or fake? Does it matter?* Keep the suspense by not revealing whether your necklace is real or fake.

2. Ask students to draw a symbol for materialism. Ask: *What "status symbols" do we see in our world today (e.g., stiletto shoes, designer purses, extravagant sweet 16 parties, bling, celebrities, etc.)? What are the positive and negative effects of materialism (the love of owning things) on a person's life?*

Read Text

1. Explain that the short story by Guy de Maupassant is said to be one of the greatest short stories ever written. It was written in 1881 published in a French newspaper. As they read, ask students to think about ways in which the story relates to our world today.

2. Distribute "The Necklace" by Guy de Maupassant. Ask students to read the text independently, or lead a scaled-down reader's theater. Students will read assigned parts of the story aloud. (*Note:* Although the story is not written as a play, it can still be read in parts if the students are savvy about following along and understand the dialogue.)

   ■ Narrator (change up every page or so)
   ■ Madame Loisel
   ■ Mr. Loisel
   ■ Madame Forestier

Text-Dependent Questions

Select from the following text-dependent questions to lead class discussion:

- In the first few paragraphs, does the author convince you to feel sorry for Madame Loisel? How does Maupassant's word choice influence you to sympathize or not sympathize for Madame Loisel? Explain with textual evidence.
- What does Madame Loisel's reaction to the invitation reveal about her character?
- What quote from Madame Loisel most reflects her character flaws?
- Contrast the descriptions de Maupassant uses to describe Madame Loisel's demeanor before and after she puts on the necklace from Madame Forestier (this can be done on a chart listing words and phrases). What point is the author trying to make?
- Madame Loisel declares, "We must consider how to replace that ornament." Is she justified in considering this as her only option? Is she being true to her character? What other options could she consider and still keep the same characterization as described by de Maupassant?
- How is the attainment of and losing the necklace representative of her dream? (Sample response: The dream that material items will bring happiness is an illusion, and when she lost the necklace, she lost the dream and lost her "life" paying for that dream.)
- How is the necklace representative of Madame Loisel's character? (Sample response: She's fake herself—she's pretty on the outside but very shallow on the inside.)
- How is the necklace representative of the upper class lifestyle? (Sample response: Even the wealthy want to portray an illusion of being wealthy.)
- To what extent is Madame Loisel motivated by fear?
- At the end of the story, do you feel sorry for Madame Loisel? Why or why not?
- Is the husband's character necessary in telling this story? Why or why not?
- Did you feel sorry for her at the beginning of the story? Typically readers feel sorry for characters in poverty. What does the author do to keep you from feeling sympathy? Why is this important?

Literary Analysis

Guide students through a literary analysis using Handout 7.1: Blank Literary Analysis Wheel. Lead students through a basic discussion of each literary element, then emphasize the interaction of the elements with more complex questions.

Students can take notes on the wheel and draw arrows to illustrate connections between concepts. Focus on the following complex questions:

- How do symbols illuminate the themes in the text?
- How does the narrator's point of view shape reader's response to the text? How does it help develop the theme?
- How does the setting influence the conflict and plot?
- How does the theme influence the way in which de Maupassant develops his characters (e.g., consider, if the theme were different, how might the resolution be different, etc.)?

The following notes are provided, but other interpretations are welcomed. Teacher may wish to discuss this as whole group, or assign small group, partner, or individual work. Some ideas below were adapted from http://www.cummings studyguides.net/Guides4/Necklace.html.

- **Context:** Written in 1881 for a French newspaper.
- **Purpose:** To entertain, to make audiences aware of materialism.
- **Themes:** Appearance versus reality, disillusionment, materialism, social status, jealousy, and pride.
- **Character:** Madame Loisel learns that she wasted her life in her desire to obtain something of value; just as the necklace was fake, so too were the people at the party who make judgments based only on appearances. Loisel is insecure and believes that the necklace will bring value to her identity.
- **Setting:** The setting of Paris, late 19th century, reflects the nature of the class system.
- **Mood:** The mood is realistic of this time, although her grief-stricken life creates a cheerless, distressing feel. Words to create this feel of her unhappy state at the beginning include "slip of fate," "shabby," "suffered," "irritated," and "grief."
- **Conflict:** Madame Loisel experiences the absence of an internal conflict. The fact that she does not consider "should I tell the truth to Madame Foriester that I lost the necklace?" reveals her fear, as well as her husband's fear about disclosure. Externally, however, she experiences conflict over her fate of working/poverty. Consider, is her circumstance a result of fate or her own choices?
- **Symbols:** The necklace can be interpreted to have multiple layers of meaning: She perceives that the necklace will have a transforming power on her life, thus the necklace represents her dream. She obtained the dream when she had the necklace and lost her dream when the necklace was lost. All the time, however, the necklace was fake, just as the dream was fake in the promise of bringing fulfillment. Madame Forestier realizes that material items are only as significant as people perceive them to be. The fake neck-

lace is symbolic of Madame Loisel's character—pretty on the outside but plain on the inside. It reflects the fake nature of even the upper class, even she wants to present the illusion that she is wealthy; the lost necklace itself represents Loisel's loss in status. Other images include the mirror emphasizing the reflection of reality to Loisel. Loisel's reflection of reality is that to be loved, admired, and beautiful, one must have nice things.

- **Tone:** The tone is rather cautionary to the reader, guarding against materialism; depending on interpretation the ending is either sympathetic or accusatory—did she get what she deserved? The author is careful to present Madame Loisel in a light for the reader to judge whether she is a victim of bad luck or her own choices.

- **Point of View:** Third-person limited—Madame Loisel. This limits the reader's understanding, keeping the reader from realizing the truth about the necklace. This contributes to the theme because the reader also engages in not realizing the "truth" until the end of the story.

- **Language:** Use of the name of where they live—Rue Martyr—is significant. A martyr is someone who sacrifices his or her life for a cause. Madame Loisel views herself as a martyr because she sacrifices her life that could have been of beauty and charm. Later when she has to work to make the money for the paste necklace, her martyrdom is exaggerated further. However, she only sees herself as the martyr when her husband is the one who has made sacrifices for her behalf. Her perception of reality is skewed in her perspective of martyrdom.

Big Idea Reflection

Use Handout 7.2: Big Idea Reflection to help students transfer knowledge of the story to real life.

- **Concepts:** Illusion, happiness, pride, wealth, social status.

- **Generalizations:** Material items are only as powerful as people perceive them to be. People mask their true selves to appear better than others. People look to material things to bring happiness and fulfillment.

- **Problem:** Do we value material things or our inner being? Fake versus real, etc.

- **Insight:** People mask their true selves to impress others. Having things will help them feel better about themselves. Maintaining or gaining social status involves consequences. In being humble in truth or satisfied with what you have, you can avoid distress.

- **World/Community/Individual:** Individual—Do I feel that my life would be more fulfilled by having "things?" To what extent do I go to obtain these material things? Community—We often judge our peers only by their appearances and not for who they are on the inside. World—Pursuing the American dream—obtaining wealth by overworking at the cost of missing out on quality time with family. We feign wealth at several levels (e.g., fake Prada purses, having expensive cars to appear to have the great life).

- **Implications/Solutions:** In what ways might I address the issues brought up by world/community/individual?

In-Class Activities to Deepen Learning

1. Assign students to work in groups of 2–3 to support evidence of the theme with specific quotes from the story. Groups should share their answers with the class. Suggested themes are: appearance versus reality, materialism, jealousy, pride, or martyrdom.
2. Ask students to read "The Paste" by Henry James (available online). This is a similar story written in reverse. Students can compare and contrast story elements and themes.
3. Conduct an improvisational talk show with a host and the following characters as guests:
   - A freed prisoner from a cave in Greece
   - Mrs. Hutchinson
   - Vincent Van Gogh
   - Charlie (old or new, but be student should be sensitive in acting as the unintelligent Charlie)
   - Madame
   - Leading expert on advice-giving (Dr. Phil-like character)
   - Participants also include members of the audience. Ideally, every student should have a part.

Assign roles and give students 5 minutes for silent thinking time. Help students prepare by asking each participant to plan for the talk show:

- **Guest characters:** Jot down ideas for answers to the questions they will be asked (what did you learn from encountering reality, how did you grow, how was your experience similar to another guest's?).
- **Audience members:** Jot down unanswered questions "The Necklace" leaves for the reader.
- **The expert:** Jot down suggestions to help Madame Loisel deal with problems of vanity and her future.
- **Host:** Prepare the order of questions and flow of the show (15–20 minute show). The host should lead a discussion such as the following: *Our guests are here today to discuss their experiences with appearance versus reality. Each guest has experienced the truth in some significant way. What*

did each of you learn from your experience in encountering truth or reality? How did you grow and what did you learn (about yourself, the world, or reality)? Was your experience similar to other guests in any way? In what ways? Later, focus questions toward Madame Loisel. Members of the audience develop unanswered questions to ask Madame Loisel and her husband (e.g., did Madame Forestier return the money to you?). Bring an expert onto the show (a Dr. Phil-type figure). The host should ask the expert to give advice to Madame Loisel.

Concept Connections

Lead students through a discussion using Handout 2.3: Concept Organizer. Students should list examples about how the work demonstrates some of the generalizations. Provide guidance as needed. Figure 7.1 provides some sample responses.

Choice-Based Differentiation Products

Students may choose one of the following independent products to complete (*Note*: Use Rubric 1: Product Rubric in Appendix C to assess student products):

- Rewrite this story as a children's story for ages 5–7. Provide two illustrations to support your story. Adapt the story by changing one element (e.g., setting, symbol, conflict, point of view, etc.).
- Write the story from a first person narrative account of Madame Forestier. Use appropriate characterization and internal conflict to develop new insight into the plot.
- Create a collage of how materialism is depicted in both the story and our society. Include at least three quotes from the text, and three quotes from other sources. Include at least five images related to the text and five images related to our world. Include a description of each item and quote on a separate sheet of paper. Also include a half-page reflection relating the theme of materialism to the theme of truth versus perception.

ELA Practice Tasks

Assign one of the following tasks as a performance-based assessment for this lesson:

- Does the author reveal Madame Loisel as a victim of fate or a victim of her own choices? In an argumentative essay, cite at least three examples from the text to support your claim. Include a counterclaim within your essay.
- Compare Madame Loisel to another character within this unit (e.g., Faye from *Flowers for Algernon*, Tessie from "The Lottery"). What generaliza-

Perception of truth* varies. (*"Truth" and "reality" can be interchanged to fit the context of the work.)
Madame Loisel mistakenly believes that the diamond necklace is real. She also denied the reality of her situation in being in the lower class and wanted to believe and feign that she was a part of the upper social class.
There are negatives and positives in realizing truth.
She is filled with regret for having to live in poverty to pay off her debt.
There are consequences to believing perception rather than the truth (truth being hidden).
In falsely believing that to be a worthy person, she needed to be rich, she lived a life motivated by a lie instead of accepting her own self and status.
Examine the relationship between truth, perception, power, ignorance, happiness, perspective, and/or freedom.
Not knowing the truth led to a life in chains, without freedom. In hiding the truth, one is succumbed to a life without freedom. She hid the truth from Mrs. Forestier until the end.

Figure 7.1. Sample student responses to truth versus perception generalizations.

tions can you make about both characters? In an explanatory essay, explain at least three similarities citing textual support in your answer.

Formative Assessment

1. Ask students to respond to the following prompt in a single paragraph: *Explain how the author uses three literary devices to contribute to the overall message of the story (e.g., point of view, symbols, language, characterization, etc.). Include at least three specific examples to support your thinking within a well-developed paragraph.*

2. Use the scoring guidelines in Figure 7.2 to evaluate students' assessments.

	Literary Analysis
0	Provides no response.
1	Response is limited and vague.
2	Response is accurate with 1–2 literary techniques described with vague connection to a main idea or theme. Response includes limited or no evidence from text.
3	Response is appropriate and accurate, describing at least three literary techniques and a main idea or theme. Response is literal and includes some evidence from the text.
4	Response is insightful and well supported, describing at least three literary techniques and the theme. Response includes abstract connections and substantial evidence from the text.

Figure 7.2. Scoring guidelines for Lesson 7 formative assessment.

Name: _____   Date: _____

Handout 7.1
Blank Literary Analysis Wheel

Directions: Draw arrows across elements to show connections.

Text: _____

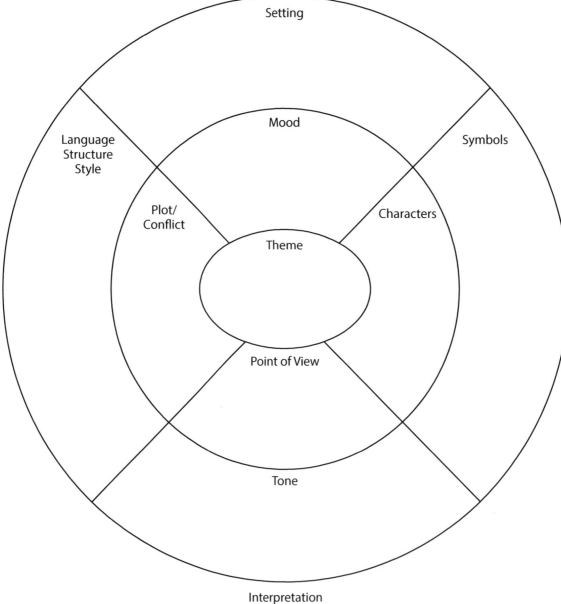

Purpose/Context

Setting

Mood

Language Structure Style

Symbols

Plot/ Conflict

Characters

Theme

Point of View

Tone

Interpretation

Created by Tamra Stambaugh, Ph.D., & Emily Mofield, Ed.D., 2015.

Name: _____   Date: _____

Handout 7.2
Big Idea Reflection

What?	**Concepts:** What concepts/ideas are in the text?	
	Generalizations: What broad statement can you make about one or more of these concepts? Make it generalizable beyond the text.	
	Issue: What is the main issue, problem, or conflict?	
So What?	**Insight:** What insight on life is provided from this text?	
	World/Community/Individual: How does this text relate to you, your community, or your world? What question does the author want you to ask yourself?	
Now What?	**Implications:** How should you respond to the ideas in the text? What action should you take? What are the implications of the text? What can you do with this information?	

Created by Emily Mofield, Ed.D., & Tamra Stambaugh, Ph.D., 2015.

TRUTH:
An Examination of How Society Is Deceived

Lesson

8

Analyzing Propaganda

Goals/Objectives

Content: To analyze and interpret literature, art, and media, students will be able to:

- evaluate how literary or visual elements impact a work's overall message,
- explain with evidence how a writer supports a claim,
- respond to interpretations of texts through a variety of contexts by justifying ideas and providing new information, and
- relate interpretations of texts to the real world.

Process: To develop thinking, reasoning, and communication skills, students will be able to:

- analyze meaning, purpose, and literary/visual elements;
- make inferences from provided evidence;
- communicate to create, express, and interpret ideas; and
- analyze primary sources (purpose, assumptions, consequences).

Concept: To understand the concept of truth in the language arts, students will be able to:

- make and defend generalizations about truth versus perception,
- explain the positives and negatives of knowing the truth,
- analyze the consequences of believing perception rather than truth, and
- explain the relationship between truth and other concepts.

Accelerated CCSS ELA Standards

SL.8.2	W.9-10.4	RI.9-10.4
SL.9-10.1	W.9-10.5	RI.9-10.5
SL.9-10.1c	RI.9-10.1	RI.9-10.6
SL.9-10.1d	RI.9-10.2	RH.9-10.1
SL.9-10.4	RI.9-10.3	RH.9-10.2

- RH.9-10.5
- RH.9-10.6
- RH.9-10.8
- RH.9-10.9

Materials

- Prints to display, available online:
  - "Uncle Sam Is Calling You" by James Flagg, 1916
  - "We Can Do it!" by J. Howard Miller, 1942
  - (Optional) "Wanted! For Murder, Her Careless Talk Cost Lives" by Victor Keppler, 1944
  - "The Poisonous Mushroom" cover, 1938

- Student copies of "The Poisonous Mushroom" by Ernst Hiemer, available at http://research.calvin.edu/german-propaganda-archive/story2.htm
- Handout 2.3: Concept Organizer (continued from previous lessons)
- Handout 8.1: Blank Rhetorical Analysis Wheel
- Blank Visual Analysis Wheel to refer to as a model (Appendix B)
- Rubric 1: Product Rubric (Appendix C)

Note: Determine whether or not the materials in this lesson are appropriate for your students. In particular, "The Poisonous Mushroom" deals with sensitive content that relates to the atrocities of the Holocaust, and as such, other primary source propaganda materials may need to be substituted.

Introductory Activities

1. Display following quote: "The distorted truth is not the truth." Ask: *How do we see this evident in our current society or history? Propaganda is used to persuade others to believe in ideas. It has been used to influence societies as a whole. Examples of this are especially found during wartime.*
2. Display examples of the following three posters in American history. Guide students to notice various aspects of each work in a whole-group discussion. Refer to the Visual Analysis Wheel by showing it on the board or projector, but is not necessary for students to complete written notes.
   - **"Uncle Sam Is Calling You" by James Flagg, 1916:** This is the most famous poster in the world, created during World War I. More than 4 million copies were printed. It was later used in World War II as well.
     - **Images/Symbols:** Stern fatherly image, will be disappointed if not obeyed.
     - **Techniques:** Main colors, prominent features.
     - **Message/Main Idea:** Join the army.

  ◆ **Point of View/Assumptions:** Don't let your country down, you are commanded to do this.
  ◆ **Conclusions:** Is the poster using the power emotion or reason to persuade? Support your answer with evidence.

▪ **"We Can Do it!" by J. Howard Miller, 1942:** This poster was created during World War II. It is also known as "Rosie the Riveter."
  • **Images/Symbols:** Attractive, strong woman, rolled up sleeves to represent hard work.
  • **Techniques:** Main colors, prominent features (patriotic blue shirt, red scarf on head, white dots similar to white stars on flag, raised eyebrow—as if to ask, are you going to join me?).
  • **Message/Main Idea:** Help your country by working like a man.
  • **Point of View/Assumptions:** Women's work in the factories will be tough, but it's doable and necessary.
  • **Conclusions:** Is the poster using the power of emotion or reason to persuade? Support your answer with evidence. (*Note:* Explain that "bandwagon" is the propaganda technique that appeals for someone wanting to be part of the group. The use of "*we* can do it" is use of bandwagon.)

▪ **(Optional) "Wanted! For Murder, Her Careless Talk Cost Lives" by Victor Keppler, 1944:** This poster was created during World War II when national security was a major concern. Leaking information about troop movements and details could be useful to the enemy. Students should analyze the poster for images/symbols, techniques, messages/ main idea, and point of view/assumptions. Ask: *Is the poster using the power of emotion or reason to persuade? Support your answer with evidence.* (*Note:* Explain the propaganda technique "loaded words." This technique uses language to appeal to a person's emotion. It can make the viewer feel fearful, excited, embarrassed, eager, etc.)

Rhetorical Analysis

1. Explain to students that the images studied thus far actually present "arguments." Each image is used to convey an idea or an "argument" that is supported by details and evidence. For the remainder of the lesson, they will look at arguments from varied perspectives through a more complex lens using the Rhetorical Analysis Wheel.
2. Guide students through the rhetorical analysis (using Handout 8.1: Blank Rhetorical Analysis Wheel) as a whole group. In a rhetorical analysis,

students will focus more on the persuasive reasoning in the documents. Emphasize specific elements first (e.g., logos, pathos, ethos, organization, techniques, and point of view), then move toward combining elements for more complexity: "What techniques does he use to develop pathos appeals; where are they placed and why?" Note the inner wheel conceptually spins so that its elements interact with each other and the outer wheel.

3. **"The Poisonous Mushroom" cover, 1938:** Show students the cover of "The Poisonous Mushroom" by Ernst Hiemer (available online) and distribute copies of the story. Use the Blank Rhetorical Analysis Wheel to evaluate the propaganda messages used from Nazi Germany. Guide students in whole-group discussion, using the following as a guide. Emphasize cultural sensitivity and how stereotyping and prejudice are spread through propaganda.

- **Context/Purpose:**
  - *What is the historical context?* The author of text is Ernst Hiemer, written in 1938, in Nazi Germany. It was written for children.
  - *What is the purpose of this medium?* To "educate" German children about the "dangers" of Jews, to spread anti-Semitism nationally.

- **Message/Claim:**
  - *What is the main claim?* Jews are poisonous to the German folk; others should be warned.

- **Point of View/Assumptions:**
  - *What are the assumptions behind the point of view of the text?* Jews are fungus. Jews are poisonous to culture. Jews are the reason for the problems of Germany and a threat to the future.

- **Logos/Techniques/Structure:**
  - What are the main arguments of the media and how are they supported? Analogy/symbol: Jews are like poisonous mushrooms. Main points: Jews can disguise themselves as good. A single mushroom (Jew) can destroy a city, village, or entire folk. Readers must tell others that Jews are the reason for misery, distress, illness, and death. Structure of argument: introduction to analogy, explanation of dangers, and urge to take action and warn others.

- **Pathos/Techniques/Structure:**
  - *How does the medium appeal to emotions?* Appeals to proud feelings—"mother praises the boy for his intelligence." Appeals to urgency to tell others about Jews being dangerous to society. Appeals to exclusivity—not everyone knows about the poisonous mushrooms, you have special information to share with others.

- **Ethos/Techniques/Structure:**
  - *Is the medium credible? How does the author develop trust?* It is very biased, from German perspective. The audience (children) may believe this is trustworthy because of the appeal to authority—"our teacher often told us about them!"

- **Implications:**
  - *What are the short- and long-term implications of this document?* This led to the persuasion of children to adopt these beliefs and project them onto their experience of reality. The author was likely praised by the Nazi government. Phrases such as, "the mother praises the boy for his intelligence" promotes the thinking that hating Jews is noble for the nation. The consequences are that the belief of anti-Semitism was rooted into the minds of children who grew to adore Hitler, join Hitler's Youth Program, and become Nazis. The adoption of these beliefs became the rationale to treat Jews as non-humans (fungus), taking away their rights, placing them into ghettos, and moving them to concentration camps.

- **Evaluation:**
  - *How effective is the author in supporting his claim? Is there too much bias or emotional manipulation? Is the claim fully supported?* The text is extremely biased and plays on emotional manipulation of children. Although points are given and supported, the text does not address an opposing point of view. Although the author supports the claim, it is not an "ethical" argument.

- **Additional background information:**
  - Several posters, books, and movies promoted anti-Semitism, including the movie *The Eternal Jew*. The story of the poisonous mushroom is only one of several other children's stories. There are archives of these sources and many are available online.

In-Class Activities to Deepen Learning

1. Make connections. Ask: *How do the ideas in this document relate to the ideas presented in "The Lottery" read previously in the unit?* (Sample response The German citizens and their children are blinded by what they are being taught—it is appropriate to hate Jews. Likewise, in "The Lottery," citizens are blinded by tradition that it is appropriate to kill one day of the year. The blame/guilt of the community must be placed on someone. For Nazi Germany, the blame for their problems was placed on the Jews.)

2. Assign students to work individually or alone to conduct a Rhetorical Analysis on another primary source related to World War II. Students should summarize their findings to the class. There are many archives online that display Nazi propaganda posters and material, such as:
   - "The Oath to Adolf Hitler," available at http://www.calvin.edu/academic/cas/gpa/hess1.htm
   - "Reality is Different; Disillusioned USA Soldiers," available at http://www.calvin.edu/academic/cas/gpa/dr05.htm
   - Leaflets from D-Day, available at http://www.calvin.edu/academic/cas/gpa/ww2leaf.htm

3. Revisit the opening quote, "The distorted truth is not the truth." Say: We have seen how Nazi Germany used this to persuade a nation. How do we see this quote in our world today? Consider advertising and politics in particular as you craft your response.

Concept Connections

Discuss connections to truth versus perception by asking the following questions. Students may reflect on concept connections using Handout 2.3: Concept Organizer, continued from previous lessons. Figure 8.1 provides some sample responses.
- What generalizations can you make regarding deceived societies? (Sample response: Ignorant societies are controlled societies. Distorted truth can be an influential, powerful force on society.)
- What benefit does it bring you to know the "truth" of media messages?

Choice-Based Differentiated Products

Students may choose one of the following independent products to complete (*Note*: Use Rubric 1: Product Rubric in Appendix C to assess student products):

Perception of truth* varies. (*"Truth" and "reality" can be interchanged to fit the context of the work.)
Viewers believe messages that distort the truth.
There are negatives and positives in realizing truth.
In knowing the truth, we can make wiser decisions. Judgment may cause one to be more cautious and aware of what is presented.
There are consequences to believing perception rather than the truth (truth being hidden).
Power sources can take advantage of those who believe in distorted truths.
Examine the relationship between truth, perception, power, ignorance, happiness, perspective, and/or freedom.
Distorted truth holds power and influence.

Figure 8.1. Sample student responses to truth versus perception generalizations.

- Conduct a visual analysis on three American WWII posters using the Blank Visual Analysis Wheel. What similarities do you notice about all three ads? What generalizations can you make from these similarities?
- Conduct a visual analysis on three advertisements that sell the same item using the Blank Visual Analysis Wheel. What similarities do you notice about all three ads? What generalizations can you make from these similarities?
- Find at least three magazine/newspaper ads that display the bandwagon technique and three magazine ads that use the loaded words technique. What is the underlying assumption behind each ad? What do these ads reveal about truth versus perception? How do these ads relate to another lesson in this unit? Write your responses in a written reflection and share your ideas with the class.

ELA Practice Tasks

Assign one of the following tasks as a performance-based assessment for this lesson:

- Examine three American propaganda posters (all from the same era). In an explanatory essay, describe how the motives behind pieces of media affect their presentation. Refer to visual and persuasive elements of the posters within your response.
- How does the media blind society from the truth? In an essay, address this question and compare today's media to Plato's Allegory. Be sure to cite specific examples from Plato's Allegory in your explanation.

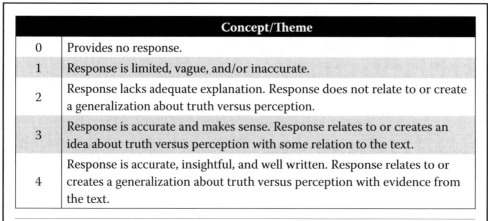

	Concept/Theme
0	Provides no response.
1	Response is limited, vague, and/or inaccurate.
2	Response lacks adequate explanation. Response does not relate to or create a generalization about truth versus perception.
3	Response is accurate and makes sense. Response relates to or creates an idea about truth versus perception with some relation to the text.
4	Response is accurate, insightful, and well written. Response relates to or creates a generalization about truth versus perception with evidence from the text.

Figure 8.2. Scoring guidelines for Lesson 8 formative assessment.

Formative Assessment

1. Ask students to respond to the following prompt in a single paragraph: *Choose one media source that is especially powerful to you today. How does it exemplify the theme of truth versus perception?*
2. Use the scoring guidelines in Figure 8.2 to evaluate students' assessments.

Name: _____   Date: _____

Handout 8.1

Blank Rhetorical Analysis Wheel

Directions: Draw arrows across elements to show connections.

Text: _____

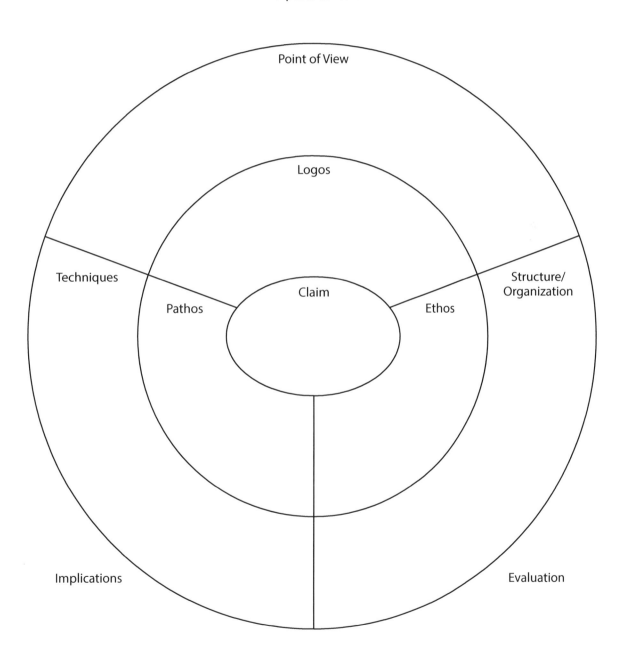

Purpose/Context

Point of View

Logos

Techniques

Claim

Pathos

Ethos

Structure/
Organization

Implications

Evaluation

Created by Emily Mofield, Ed.D., & Tamra Stambaugh, Ph.D., 2015.

Lesson

9

Fahrenheit 451
by Ray Bradbury

Goals/Objectives

Content: To analyze and interpret literature, art, and media, students will be able to:

- evaluate how literary or visual elements impact a work's overall message,
- respond to interpretations of texts through a variety of contexts by justifying ideas and providing new information,
- analyze how an individual's motivation and behavior are revealed, and
- relate interpretations of texts to the real world.

Process: To develop thinking, reasoning, and communication skills, students will be able to:

- analyze meaning, purpose, and literary/visual elements;
- make inferences from provided evidence;
- reason through an issue (points of view, assumptions, implications); and
- communicate to create, express, and interpret ideas.

Concept: To understand the concept of truth in the language arts, students will be able to:

- make and defend generalizations about truth versus perception,
- explain the positives and negatives of knowing the truth,
- analyze the consequences of believing perception rather than truth, and
- explain the relationship between truth and other concepts.

Accelerated CCSS ELA Standards

- RL.9-10.1
- RL.9-10.2
- RL.9-10.3
- RL.9-10.4
- RL.9-10.5

- SL.9-10.1
- SL.9-10.1c
- SL.9-10.1d
- W.9-10.4
- W.9-10.5

Materials

- Student copies of *Fahrenheit 451* by Ray Bradbury
- "Ray Bradbury's *Fahrenheit 451* Audio Guide," available at http://www. neabigread.org/books/fahrenheit451/media
- Butcher paper/markers
- Cutouts of prereading
- Sticky notes (about 20 per student)
- Handout 2.3: Concept Organizer
- Handout 9.1: *Fahrenheit 451* Reading Guide
- Handout 9.2: *Fahrenheit 451* Symbol Guide
- Student copies of Blank Literary Analysis Wheel, Big Idea Reflection, and Reasoning About a Situation or Event (see Appendix B) as needed
- Rubric 1: Product Rubric (Appendix C)
- Teacher's Guide to Handout 9.2 (Appendix D)

Note: Parts of the novel include adult language. It may be best to get parent permission before assigning the novel. This novel may be appropriate only for older middle school students.

Introductory Activities

1. Ask students to imagine waking up to a world where no books were allowed (including e-books, informational texts, and online reading sources). Say: *Text is still allowed on billboards and on items (cola cans, etc.), but not in books. Write a first person journal entry about your experience (what you think caused banned books, why, and how you feel about it).* Students may wish to share their responses with the class.

2. **Engage students in a quick debate.** Ask students if they agree or disagree with the following statements. Students may stand on one side of the room for "agree" and the other side of the room for "disagree." Call on students to discuss their reasoning.
   - Some books should be banned.
   - The government has the right to censor material to protect the general public.
   - The television has negative effects on American society.
   - Technology isolates the individual.
   - Ignorance is bliss.

3. Distribute the following words and phrases (written on sticky notes or index cards). Each student should have one word/phrase. Students will create a

story as a class about what they predict the book will be about. Start off the story by saying: *Once upon a time there was a man named Montag. He . . . .* Then have the next student add to the story. The student must incorporate the word/phrase in some way. The student should say more than one sentence. After the story is over, ask students to be aware of these words/phrases as they read the story. They all are very significant or symbolic in some way.

- Pigeon-winged books
- To everything there is a season
- Harvard degrees on the tracks
- The salamander devours his tail
- He meets Clarisse
- Half out of the cave
- Dentrifice! Dentrifice! Dentrifice!
- Time has fallen asleep in the afternoon sunshine
- Black cobra
- Phoenix
- Great python
- 451 degrees Fahrenheit
- Heath and the Salamander
- Sand
- Burning Bright
- Mechanical hound
- Cheshire cats
- Man in the moon
- Mildred
- It was burning, it was warming

In-Class Activities to Deepen Learning (During Reading)

1. Distribute Handout 9.1: *Fahrenheit 451* Reading Guide, which details activities for students to complete while reading the novel, and Handout 9.2: *Fahrenheit 451* Symbol Guide (a teacher's guide to this handout is provided; see Appendix D). Assign reading sections as you see appropriate for your students. Depending on the pace of student reading, develop small groups based on student reading progress.
2. Students can work in literature groups to discuss their journal responses, list of symbols, quote responses, etc. Students should ask each other questions, agree and disagree with each other, and be naturally interactive.

3. (Optional) If additional structure is needed, you may also wish to assign the following rotating roles, although you may want to be careful balancing the work load for students:

  ▪ **Insights on Life:** Finds quotes that reveal specific insights/lessons on life.

  ▪ **Realization Reader:** Finds realizations throughout the text of various characters.

  ▪ **Conflict Counter:** Finds evidence of dilemmas encountered between and within characters

  ▪ **Question Maker:** Develops a list of five questions to ask various characters.

4. Conduct a whole class Socratic Seminar on Parts 1 and 2 of the novel. Use the following questions to guide discussion:

  ▪ Round robin: Use 1–3 words to describe the society portrayed in *Fahrenheit 451.*

  ▪ Agree or disagree? The people's indifference was caused by the government. Cite textual evidence. (*Note:* Be sure to point out Beatty on p. 58: "There you have it, it didn't come from the government down. . . it came from . . . ." Government control of people's lives was not a conspiracy of dictators or tyrants, but a consensus of everyday people.)

  ▪ "Faber the public itself stopped reading on its own accord!" What does this reveal about the society?

  ▪ What does this indifference lead to (in the novel and in real life)? (Sample response: A self-focused society, entertainment focus, no value for human life.)

  ▪ How are Montag's indifferences shattered? How does he react to the apathy around him?

  ▪ How does the following quote relate to the people in Montag's society? "The mechanical hound slept but did not sleep, lived but did not live in its gently humming, gently vibrating, softly illuminated kennel back in a dark corner of the firehouse (p. 24) . . . . It doesn't think anything we don't want it to think (p. 27)." (Sample response: The mechanical hound is a metaphor for Montag and other members of his society who live, yet do not live and who think only what the TV tells them to think.)

  ▪ Agree or disagree? People are weak-minded; they don't want to think for themselves and solve the troubling problems of the world. Give an example from the book/our world.

  ▪ What happens when we are afraid to think? (Sample response: They fear the thought of knowing, which leads them to depend on others to think for them. Because they aren't thinking, they need something to occupy their time.)

■ What are the consequences for a society that is consumed in indifference, entertainment, and ignorance? (Sample response: In a world where people do not think for themselves, they depend on others such as the government to think for them. When people are distracted by their own self desires or entertainment, they become disinterested in the affairs around them and can be easily controlled. Ignorant societies are controlled societies.)

■ Agree or disagree? "It is far easier to live a life of seclusion and illusion—a life where the television is reality." (*Note:* This should remind students of Plato's Allegory and *Flowers for Algernon*.)

■ Discuss the following quotes:
  • Page 61: "We're the happiness boys . . . . " How does this relate to a previous novel, lesson, or concept?
  • Page 74: "Maybe the books can get us halfway out of the cave." How?
  • Page 78: The distraction of "Dendham's Dentrifice"—why is distraction significant in this novel and to the broader themes of this unit?

■ Is it better to live in ignorance but be happy, or to live with the hurtful truth? Have students individually write their responses.

Concept Connections (During Reading)

1. Write the three truth versus perception generalizations each on their own piece of butcher paper:
   ■ Perception of truth varies.
   ■ There are negatives and positives in realizing truth.
   ■ There are consequences to believing perception (appearances) rather than the truth.

Divide the class into three groups. Assign groups to a generalization. Students should write examples of how three characters experience the assigned generalization. Have students then share with the class. For example, how did Montag, Clarisse, and Mildred experience "Perception of truth varies"?

2. Share "Ray Bradbury's *Fahrenheit 451* Audio Guide." Students should listen to Bradbury speak and develop a list of three questions they would have liked to ask him (he died in 2012).

In-Class Activities to Deepen Learning (After Reading)

1. Discuss the following question: *Could the world depicted in* Fahrenheit 451 *be a reality for us today? In what ways does it mirror our society?*
2. Using Reasoning About a Situation or Event, analyze "Is ignorance bliss?" from multiple character perspectives (e.g., Montag, Mildred, the government, and Granger). Figure 9.1 provides some sample responses.

Literary Analysis (After Reading)

Lead students through completing Blank Literary Analysis Wheel (parts may be completed in small groups or in pairs). Lead students through a basic discussion of each literary element, then emphasize the interaction of the elements with more complex questions. Encourage students to cite textual evidence throughout discussion. Students can take notes on the wheel and draw arrows to illustrate connections between concepts. The following notes are provided, but other interpretations are welcomed. Emphasize the interaction of literary elements throughout and encourage students to cite textual evidence.

- **Context:** Written during the Cold War, after World War II (1953). While the book presents a message about government censorship, this was only part of Bradbury's purpose. Bradbury had fears that TV would harm American society. He felt that people would no longer read literature with the presence of the TV. In the novel, Bradbury warns America of a world where indifference and self-fulfillment can destroy a culture.
- **Purpose:** To entertain, to present a mirror into our own society.
- **Themes:** Themes relate to truth versus perception, censorship, true happiness, etc.
- **Character:** Montag learns happiness is in appreciating the human experience of engaging in critical thought. He considers "How can I find a meaningful life?"
- **Setting:** The setting is a 24th-century city—this challenges the reader to think about the possibilities of the future if current trends of contemporary society continue; the beginning of novel is autumn, which represents change is coming.
- **Mood:** Sometimes hostile, threatening, suspenseful.
- **Conflict:** Montag's main internal conflict is "Am I happy?"
- **Symbols:** Review the symbol chart. Symbols include pigeon-winged books, white imagery, machine imagery (mechanical hound), carnival imagery (masks), mirror, Phoenix, Hearth and the Salamander, Sieve and the Sand.
- **Point of View:** Third person limited allows the reader to sympathize with Montag; his point of view about the world illuminates the themes.

Stakeholders	Montag	Mildred	Government	Granger
Point of View	No. He didn't realize he was in ignorance; he longs to know the truth found in books.	Yes. She is content in her self-satisfying life but doesn't realize she is living such a fraudulent life.	Yes. It wants people to live in ignorance and indifference to gain control.	No. He knows that ignorance is not bliss; is like the freed prisoner in Plato's "Allegory of the Cave."
Assumptions	Happiness will come in realizing the truth.	Ignorance is bringing a temporary sense of self-satisfaction. If people don't have books they will not have critical thought to question the government.	People aren't smart enough to question government motives.	If he can help people like Montag there is hope for society.
Implications	Begins a journey of self-discovery out of the cave.	She does not know how to truly love and appreciate people in her life or the experience of living.	Takes control over an apathetic society, does not value human life.	Brings people to the tracks to preserve society.

Figure 9.1. *Is ignorance bliss?* Sample chart.

- **Language:** There are numerous metaphors throughout. Consider use of contrasting imagery in describing Clarisse versus Mildred. Consider use of names—Clarisse (clear), Stoneman and Black, Mildred (MILD red), etc.

Big Idea Reflection (After Reading)

Use the Big Idea Reflection (see Appendix B) to help students transfer knowledge of the novel to real life.

- **Concepts:** Identity, happiness, control, power, indifference, apathy, knowledge, freedom.

- **Generalizations:** Truth brings freedom; ignorance is not bliss; happiness comes from knowledge; censorship sets conditions for control (consider the similarities between censorship and propaganda—keeping one from doing something versus encouraging one to do something).
- **Problem:** Societal indifference, societal ignorance, government control, etc.
- **Insight:** This is a warning against indifference and apathy. An ignorant society is a controlled society. Happiness is not from self-satisfaction. Critical thought is important for a society. We can be "played" without realizing it (relates to propaganda lesson).
- **World/Community/Individual:** Individual—Am I happy? Do I care? Am I controlled by others because I am apathetic? Community—We have hundreds of friends on Facebook, but are they meaningful relationships? Entertainment dominates our culture and distracts us from critical thought and from really knowing the truth in the world. World—The decline of valuing human life; the absence of critical thought, the shallow lives lived with shallow relationships.
- **Implications/Solutions:** How might we address some of these issues?

Concept Connections (After Reading)

Discuss appearance versus reality or truth versus perception concept generalizations. Students may work as pairs or individuals to complete their thoughts on Handout 2.3: Concept Organizer, continued from previous lessons. Figure 9.2 provides some sample responses.

Choice-Based Differentiated Products

Students may choose one of the following independent products to complete (*Note:* Use Rubric 1: Product Rubric in Appendix C to assess student products unless otherwise instructed):

- Write a comparison essay comparing Plato's "Allegory of the Cave" to *Fahrenheit 451*. Use at least three quotes from each work to support your arguments (see Rubric 2: Comparison Essay).
- Think of how you see elements of *Fahrenheit 451* in today's world. Create a visual collage with quotes, words, newspaper articles, and pictures to reveal these similarities. Turn in your collage as well as a written description explaining the elements on your collage and how they relate to *Fahrenheit 451*. Use specific examples from the book to support your symbols in explaining how our world and *Fahrenheit 451* are related (see Rubric 3: Collage Rubric).

Perception of truth* varies. (*"Truth" and "reality" can be interchanged to fit the context of the work.)
People in society believe in the world that is presented to them, never questioning authority. They believe lies such as Benjamin Franklin was the first fireman to start fires.
There are negatives and positives in realizing truth.
Montag's journey toward understanding truth involves his house being burned, him questioning his life, job, and marriage. He finds new life with the dust-jackets.
There are consequences to believing perception rather than the truth (truth being hidden).
Montag's society never knew the truth about their own history or government, so they never questioned it. An ignorant society is a controlled society. Power/authority can take advantage of the vulnerable and ignorant. The people of society, however, are content in their ignorance.
Examine the relationship between truth, perception, power, ignorance, happiness, perspective, and/or freedom.
Ignorance of truth leaves a society vulnerable to power.

Figure 9.2. Sample student responses to truth versus perception generalizations.

- Think of the unanswered questions the book leaves. Write a follow-up chapter to the end of the book. Include at least four elements of figurative language (highlight or underline these). Use the style and tone Bradbury uses. Create a title for your story.

- The novel illuminates many current issues of today including privacy and censorship. What ethical issues today relate to these concepts (e.g., ad tracking on Facebook, Google tracking to sell personal data to advertisers or even insurance companies, the government being able to track your phone calls and possibly Internet activity)? Where is the line between security and freedom? What is your viewpoint? Write an editorial, a letter to a legislator, or a mock bill to show your viewpoint one of these issues.

ELA Practice Tasks

Assign one of the following tasks as a performance-based assessment for this lesson:

- How does Bradbury use symbolism to illuminate "fiction reveals truth that reality obscures?" Answer within a well-developed essay citing examples from the text.

Literary Analysis	
0	Provides no response.
1	Response is limited and vague.
2	Response is accurate with 1–2 literary techniques described with vague connection to a main idea or theme. Response includes limited or no evidence from text.
3	Response is appropriate and accurate, describing at least three literary techniques and a main idea or theme. Response is literal and includes some evidence from the text.
4	Response is insightful and well supported, describing at least three literary techniques and the theme. Response includes abstract connections and substantial evidence from the text.

Figure 9.3. Scoring guidelines for Lesson 9 formative assessment.

- Compare Mildred from *Fahrenheit 451* to Madame Loisel in "The Necklace." What generalizations can you make about both of them? Cite sufficient examples from both texts to support your answer in an expository essay.
- In *Fahrenheit 451*, which character is most like the "freed prisoner" in Plato's Allegory? Explain your answer in a well-developed essay citing evidence from the text.
- Which character most influenced Montag's change? In an essay, develop your argument by citing examples from the novel to defend your answer.

Formative Assessment

1. Ask students to respond to the following prompt in a single paragraph: *Explain how Bradbury uses three literary devices to contribute to the overall message of the book (e.g., point of view, irony, symbols, foreshadowing, allusions, characterization, etc.) Include at least three specific examples to support your thinking.*
2. Use the scoring guidelines in Figure 9.3 to evaluate students' assessments.

Handout 9.1
Fahrenheit 451 Reading Guide

1. Record instances of at least five theme references to appearance versus reality/ truth versus perception. List the page number and write the quote. Reflect: What is Montag learning and how is this similar to the freed prisoner in Plato's "Allegory of the Cave"?
2. Record at least five instances in which characters display indifference. How does this relate to our world today?
3. Maintain a quote response page. Find at least five quotes throughout the book that relate to an insight on life or reveal human nature.

Quote	Insight on Life

4. On Handout 9.2: *Fahrenheit 451* Symbol Guide, maintain a list of symbols and what you think they represent. On this sheet, you may also indicate if the symbol is also used to demonstrate foreshadowing, irony, or an allusion. You may go back and determine if the symbols were foreshadowing devices; this may come after reading. Support your ideas with textual evidence when possible.
5. Create a symbol for five characters in the book. Explain why you chose this symbol and support your choice with a quote from the text.

Handout 9.2
Fahrenheit 451 Symbol Guide

Directions: Indicate the meaning of each symbol. Also determine if the symbol has other literary significance (foreshadowing, irony, allusion, characterization, etc.). If the symbol is referenced later, indicate the instance.

Symbol	Meaning	Other Literary Significance	Later Reference(s)
Pigeon-winged books	Freedom: Books/ knowledge bring free-dom to the mind (as birds are free to fly).		
Hearth and the Salamander			
Sieve and the Sand			
White imagery			
Machine imag-ery (Mechanical Hound)			
Carnival imagery (masks)			
Mirror			

Name: _____ Date: _____

Symbol	Meaning	Other Literary Significance	Later Reference(s)
Phoenix			

Lesson

10

The McDonaldization of Society
by George Ritzer

Goals/Objectives

Content: To analyze and interpret literature, art, and media, students will be able to:

- explain with evidence how a writer supports a claim,
- respond to interpretations of texts through a variety of contexts by justifying ideas and providing new information,
- analyze how an individual's motivation and behavior are revealed, and
- relate interpretations of texts to the real world.

Process: To develop thinking, reasoning, and communication skills, students will be able to:

- analyze meaning, purpose, and literary/visual elements;
- make inferences from provided evidence;
- reason through an issue (points of view, assumptions, implications); and
- communicate to create, express, and interpret ideas.

Concept: To understand the concept of truth in the language arts, students will be able to:

- make and defend generalizations about truth versus perception,
- explain the positives and negatives of knowing the truth,
- analyze the consequences of believing perception rather than truth, and
- explain the relationship between truth and other concepts.

Accelerated CCSS ELA Standards

SL.9-10.1	W.9-10.5	RI.9-10.6
SL.9-10.1c	RI.9-10.1	
SL.9-10.1d	RI.9-10.2	
SL.9-10.4	RI.9-10.3	
W.9-10.4	RI.9-10.4	

Materials

- Student copies of "The McDonaldization of Society: Introduction to Sociology" by Robert Keel, available at http://www.umsl.edu/~keelr/010/mcdonsoc.html
- Handout 10.1: McDonaldization of Society Chart
- Handout 10.2: Reasoning About a Situation or Event
- (Optional) Big Idea Reflection Handout (Appendix B)

Introductory Activities

1. **Engage students in a quick debate.** Ask: *Does technology enhance or hurt human relationships? Does technology enhance or hurt the experience of being human?*
2. Bring in a McDonald's bag. In the bag put in a fake flower/rose, a piece of fruit, a homemade paper snowflake, and a handwritten letter. Do not show these items to the students until later in the lesson. Sometimes the McDonald's bags will have slogans. Discuss the text on the bag and discuss the marketing strategy and its relationship to the theme of truth versus perception (it looks good, tastes good, etc., but McDonald's is not good for you). Discuss "I'm lovin' it." Ask: *Why do people love McDonald's?* (Sample responses: It's fast, efficient, predictable, etc.)

Read Text

1. Distribute "The McDonaldization of Society: Introduction to Sociology" by Robert Keel. This is a summary of a popular book by George Ritzer, an influential sociologist. His idea of the McDonaldization of society is based on four principles, which lead to the irrationality of rationality (we think what we're doing is reasonable, but it's not). He has related an analogy of how society runs like McDonald's. This theory was developed in the 1990s; students may see how the theory is even more applicable to present society.
2. Distribute Handout 10.1: McDonaldization of Society Chart. As students read, students should summarize Ritzer's concepts.

Text-Dependent Questions

Select from the following text-dependent questions for a Socratic seminar or class discussion:

- What is meant by "the irrationality of rationality?" (Sample response: We think that these concepts help our lives, but they actually take away from the human experience.)
- What is Ritzer's main claim? (Sample response: Rational systems lead to irrational outcomes; what makes sense to make our lives easier isn't really helping us experience life.)
- What evidence is most compelling in advancing his arguments?
- Based on the evidence given in the article, which theme (e.g., predictability, calculability, etc.) do you think is most evident in our lives?
- Are there parts of his argument that you disagree with? Explain.
- This theory was developed in the 1990s. What aspects of his idea are now outdated? In what ways do you see even more evidence of McDonaldization?

In-Class Activities to Deepen Learning

1. After reading, students should work with partners to list other examples in our world. Additionally, students may reflect back on *Fahrenheit 451* for additional examples. If students did not read *Fahrenheit 451* in this unit, then focus only on real-world examples. Conduct a whole-group discussion, asking students to share examples. Ask: *What symbol would you choose to represent each principle of McDonaldization?*

2. Use Handout 10.2: Reasoning About a Situation or Event to evaluate the situation "Do rational systems deny the basic nature of being human?" Figure 10.1 provides possible responses.

3. (Optional) Revisit the McDonald's bag. Pull out each object. Each object represents a way to counter McDonaldization. Ask: *How do you think the object symbolizes a way to counter McDonaldization?*
   - **Snowflake:** Uniqueness; counters predictability; savor the "unique" shops instead of giant superstores such as Wal-Mart.
   - **Rose:** Take time to smell the roses; counters efficiency; sometimes making a cake from scratch is more enjoyable and authentic than making it from the box.
   - **Letter:** Nontechnology; counters technology; sometimes a handwritten letter is more meaningful than a text or an e-mail.
   - **Fresh fruit:** Quality over quantity; counters calculability; there are more quality vitamins in this fruit than an entire meal at McDonald's. Think about the things in life where less is really more.

4. Show the video "Globalization," available at https://www.youtube.com/watch?v=t6gwfMBkWQU. This depicts Van Gogh's *Starry Night* being destroyed by the preponderance of global markets and predictability Ask:

146

Stakeholders	Consumers	Businesses	Agree (Yes)	Disagree (No)
Point of View	Yes and no—are within the system and rely on the four principles for an easier life.	No—the efficiency, etc. brings profit. Consumers appeal to the principles of McDonald-ization.	Yes—quality is traded for quantity, etc.	No—People are more human because they have more time to experience being human.
Assumptions	Life will be better with these principles.	Money drives all endeavors and McDonald-ized principles are tools for profit.	Society is better without these systems.	The four principles benefit us.
Implications	Continue to feed into the system, thereby strengthening it.	Continue to strengthen the system by making money.	Strive to find ways to be fascinated in the mystery of being human even within the McDonald's society since it cannot be escaped.	They may live their lives robotically without realizing it.

Figure 10.1. *Do rational systems deny the basic nature of being human?* Sample responses.

What does this video suggest? You may also show YouTube videos of George Ritzer being interviewed about McDonaldization.

5. Divide students into groups. Assign a group to each principle of McDonaldization: calculability, efficiency, predictability, and technology. Ask groups to develop a skit displaying how their principle is present in our world. The class can guess which principle is represented.

Concept Connections

Lead students through a discussion about appearance versus reality and truth versus perception, using the following questions. Students may use Handout 2.3: Concept Organizer (continued from previous lessons). Figure 10.2 provides some sample responses.

Perception of truth* varies. **(*"Truth" and "reality" can be interchanged to fit the context of the work.)**
Rationality of irrationality: We believe our advancements enhance our lifestyles when in reality the advancements take away from our very human experience.
There are negatives and positives in realizing truth.
In understanding the principle of McDonaldization, it is still difficult to make changes within a society so driven by its principles. Although we understand, it is difficult to change.
There are consequences to believing perception rather than the truth (truth being hidden).
We live our lives robotically rather than embracing the full human experience. We are blinded in thinking efficiency, calculability, predictability, and technology only positively enhance our lives, when they actually have a negative effect (Ritzer's perspective). We, like those in *Fahrenheit 451* and the cave prisoners, may be content in our ignorance.
Examine the relationship between truth, perception, power, ignorance, happiness, perspective, and/or freedom.
Knowledge of truth brings freedom and power to control our own lives even within a McDonaldized system.

Figure 10.2. Sample student responses to truth versus perception generalizations.

- How does "McDonaldization" relate to Plato's "Allegory of the Cave"? (Guide students to understand that the irrationality of rationality—we are living within a system that is taking away from our experience of being human without us even realizing it. We are living in the shadows thinking that we are experiencing "life," but the four concepts are keeping us from experiencing the mysteries, excitement, and quality in relationships and experiences.)
- How does "McDonaldization" relate to *Fahrenheit 451*? (Sample response: Ignorant and indifferent societies are controlled societies. If McDonaldization puts us on autopilot, then we get away from thinking for ourselves and experiencing the pure emotions of being human. Characters in *Fahrenheit 451* were afraid to "feel" emotion and were certainly ignorant and indifferent.)
- "What we call reality is an agreement that people have arrived at to make life more livable."—Louise Nevelson. How does this quote relate to the article?
- How does this text relate to the truth versus perception generalizations and what new generalizations can be made?

Choice-Based Differentiated Products

Students may choose one of the following independent products to complete (*Note*: Use Rubric 1: Product Rubric in Appendix C to assess student products):

- Write an editorial to be submitted to your local newspaper. Explain to the public the premise of McDonaldization, discuss your opinion about the effects of McDonaldization on society, and propose ways society members can preserve the human experience within a McDonaldized world.
- Keep a record of all the ways you experience the four principles of McDonaldization within a 24-hour period. Reflect: What were the positive and negative aspects you experienced? Do you agree with Ritzer? Has McDonaldization gone too far?
- Think like a sociologist in terms of how McDonalidization affects a social institution. Consider a specific facet of society (government, religion, education, family) and describe how McDonaldization is evidenced in at least four ways. Write this in an essay format.
- Create a song about McDonaldization. Describe the four principles within your song and perform it to the class.
- Create an action plan for ways to de-McDonaldize society. In what ways might we promote more of a human experience within our society? Your action plan may be a video, brochure, pamphlet, PowerPoint, editorial, or a product of your choice. Include at least eight ways to de-McDonaldize society.

ELA Practice Tasks

Assign one of the following tasks as a performance-based assessment for this lesson:

- Has McDonaldization gone too far? Address the question in an editorial and defend your position with examples from the text and your own experience.
- How do the characters in *Fahrenheit 451* experience McDonaldization? In an essay, provide examples of the five themes of McDonaldization, citing specific examples from both texts.

Formative Assessment

1. Ask students to respond to the following prompt in a single paragraph: *"Most specifically, irrationality means that rational systems are unreasonable systems . . . . they deny the basic humanity, the human reason, or the people who work within or are served within them."* What does this suggest about an individual's conflict in the context of McDonaldization?
2. Use the scoring guidelines in Figure 10.3 to evaluate students' assessments.

Inference From Evidence	
0	Provides no response.
1	Response is limited, vague, and/or inaccurate.
2	Response is accurate, but lacks adequate explanation. Response includes some justification for either the character's motivation or conflict.
3	Response is accurate and makes sense. Response includes some justification about the character's motivation and conflict.
4	Response is accurate, insightful, interpretive, and well written. Response includes thoughtful justification about the character's motivation and conflict.

Figure 10.3. Scoring guidelines for Lesson 10 formative assessment.

Name: _____ Date: _____

Handout 10.1

McDonaldization of Society Chart

Directions: List examples of the five principles for each category.

	The McDonaldization of Society by George Ritzer	Other Examples in Our World
Efficiency Least amount of cost/effort.		
Calculability Emphasis on things that can be calculated, counted, quantified. Quantification refers to a tendency to emphasize quantity rather than quality.		
Predictability The attempt to structure our environment so that surprise and different-ness do not encroach upon our sensibilities.		

Handout 10.1, Continued

	The McDonaldization of Society by George Ritzer	Other Examples in Our World
Control Through Technology Skills and capabilities of the human are quickly becoming things of the past. Who we are and how we interact is becoming defined by our dependence upon the machine.		
The Irrationality of Rationality "Most specifically, irrationality means that rational systems are unreasonable systems. By that I mean that they deny the basic humanity, the human reason, of the people who work within or are served by them." It would make sense that these things help us, but they don't.		

Consider: What could the lasting effects of McDonaldization be on our society?

Handout 10.2
Reasoning About a Situation or Event

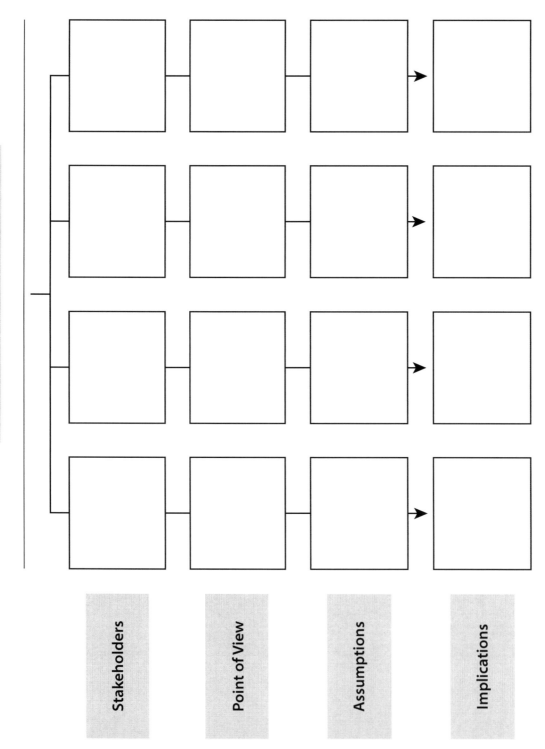

What Is the Situation?

Stakeholders

Point of View

Assumptions

Implications

Lesson

"Tell all the truth but tell it slant"
by Emily Dickinson

Goals/Objectives

Content: To analyze and interpret literature, art, and media, students will be able to:

- evaluate how literary or visual elements impact a work's overall message,
- respond to interpretations of texts through a variety of contexts by justifying ideas and providing new information, and
- relate interpretations of texts to the real world.

Process: To develop thinking, reasoning, and communication skills, students will be able to:

- analyze meaning, purpose, and literary/visual elements;
- make inferences from provided evidence; and
- communicate to create, express, and interpret ideas.

Concept: To understand the concept of truth in the language arts, students will be able to:

- make and defend generalizations about truth versus perception,
- explain the positives and negatives of knowing the truth,
- analyze the consequences of believing perception rather than truth, and
- explain the relationship between truth and other concepts.

Accelerated CCSS ELA Standards

- RL.9-10.1
- RL.9-10.2
- RL.9-10.4
- SL.9-10.1
- SL.9-10.1c
- SL.9-10.1d
- W.9-10.4

- W.9-10.5

Materials

- Student copies of "Tell all the truth but tell it slant" by Emily Dickinson, available at http://www.poetryfoundation.org/poem/247292
- Handout 2.3: Concept Organizer, continued from previous lessons
- Handout 11.1: Blank Literary Analysis Wheel
- Handout 11.2: Big Idea Reflection
- Rubric 1: Product Rubric (Appendix C)

Introductory Activities

1. As this is the last lesson in the unit, ask student to write a simile for truth (e.g., "Truth is like _____ because _____"). (Sample response: Truth is like Sour Patch candy because it can be sour and sweet at the same time.)
2. **Engage students in a quick debate.** Revisit some statements encountered at the beginning of the unit. Ask students if they have changed their perspectives.
   - It is best to know the truth.
   - Truth brings a person to freedom.
   - Truth is reality.
   - Ignorance is bliss.

Read Text

1. Ask students to read "Tell all the truth but tell it slant" and then lead them through a close reading of the text.
2. (Optional) Cut a copy of the poem into four sections (couplets). Ask students to try to piece the poem together. You may ask students to justify their reasoning for the order. Then, show students the actual order of the poem.

Text-Dependent Questions

Select from the following text-dependent questions for a Socratic seminar or class discussion:
- What is meant by "tell it slant"? Is it "kind" to tell the truth slant?
- What paradoxes can you find within the poem (e.g., too much truth blinds one from seeing any truth, infirm delight, slant truth isn't the whole truth, so how is this "all" truth?)?
- What is meant by "success in circuit lies"? (Sample response: Success comes in circling around the truth rather than directly exposing the truth.) What effect does the word "lies" have on the meaning of the poem and the inter-

pretation for the reader? (Sample response: If success comes in circling around the truth, then is it really truth, or is it a lie? "Lies" may be considered a pun. To help kinesthetically demonstrate the concept, ask students to stand up and walk in a circle around "truth.")

- What is Dickinson's attitude toward truth (positive or negative)? Where in the poem does Dickinson shift her tone toward the subject of truth from negative to positive? What effect does capitalization have on the effect of the poem? How do the capitalized words relate to the concept of truth?

- What effect does the word choice "dazzle" have on the theme of the poem?

- What is meant by "infirm Delight"? (Sample response: A weakened form of happiness, we want to know the truth, but it is not always good.)

- Is Dickinson's message to tell the whole truth gradually or to tell only part of the truth? Is "part of the truth" the same as "truth?"

- What patterns do you notice within the poem? (Sample response: Patterns of "light" imagery.)

- Imagine Emily Dickinson is a student in this class and is asked to create a simile for truth as you did at the beginning of this lesson. She is saying truth is like lightning. What would be her explanation?

- How does Dickinson's use of consonance (repetition of "s" sound) enhance the meaning of the poem? (Sample response: Truth must be told smoothly, and the "s" sound reinforces this idea. Furthermore, the slithering "s" sound makes one think of a serpent. This could be an allusion to the biblical serpent that questioned Eve: "Did God really say to not eat of this fruit?" The serpent questioned "truth" just as the poem questions the nature of truth.)

- How is the poem itself symbolic of "truth" to the reader? (Sample response: At first glance, the poem may be too difficult to understand, "blinding" the reader from knowing its message, but after gradually studying it, it is dazzling and helps us understand the real "Truth" of the poem. Poetry often goes around [circuits] a big idea to help readers better appreciate the big idea.)

- Would Dickinson agree with Plato that it is best to know the truth?

Literary Analysis

1. Conduct a scaled-down literary analysis using Handout 11.1: Blank Literary Analysis Wheel. Characters and setting may not be applicable. Point of view may be interpreted as Dickinson's point of view.

2. Focus on the following complex questions:
   - How does language contribute to the theme?
   - How do sound devices enhance symbolism?
   - How is conflict established through language?

3. The following notes may be helpful in guiding students through the analysis:
   - **Theme:** Handle truth with care.
   - **Language/Style:** Note the use of consonance, paradoxical language, capitalization, pun (lies).
   - **Symbols:** Lightning, light imagery, allusion to "serpent" through consonance "s."
   - **Conflict:** Truth versus half-truth or sudden truth versus gradual truth.
   - **Tone:** Informing or didactic.

In-Class Activities to Deepen Learning

1. Have students recreate the poem in text message form in contemporary language. Consider using emojis. Or, have students create bumper stickers with pithy messages to portray the idea of the poem.
2. Divide the class into four groups. Students may choose the group or you may assign them.
   - **Group 1:** Students show an interpretation of the poem in a creative way (they can present a skit and can adapt it so that it not just a literal depiction of the poem). Students may also present their interpretation as a frozen tableau.
   - **Group 2:** Students choose a letter of Dickinson's (first or last) name. Students write the letter on their paper and use this as a basis to create a visual depicting their interpretation of the poem (e.g., a student may draw an "L" and shape it in the form of lightning to represent the meaning of the poem).
   - **Group 3:** Students take on the role of another character or person studied within this unit and engage in discussion about how the poem relates to his or her experience. This can be done in a group talk show format like "The View."
   - **Group 4:** Students complete the Big Idea Reflection (Handout 11.2) in small groups.

Concept Connections

Discuss connections to truth versus perception generalizations. Students may reflect on concept connections using Handout 2.3: Concept Organizer, continued from previous lessons. Figure 11.1 provides some sample responses.

Perception of truth* varies. (*"Truth" and "reality" can be interchanged to fit the context of the work.)
One's perception of this truth will be difficult to take in unless the truth is offered gradually.
There are negatives and positives in realizing truth.
If all truth is given too quickly, one may be blinded from the truth or even from ever experiencing the truth at all.
There are consequences to believing perception rather than the truth (truth being hidden).
When truth hurts too much, then one will not want to know the truth at all.
Examine the relationship between truth, perception, power, ignorance, happiness, perspective, and/or freedom.
Knowledge of truth must come slowly and be delivered responsibly.

Figure 11.1. Sample student responses to truth versus perception generalizations.

Choice-Based Differentiated Products

Students may choose one of the following independent products to complete (*Note*: Use Rubric 1: Product Rubric in Appendix C to assess student products):

- Develop your own poem about truth. Use the same rhyme scheme and structure of Dickinson's poem. Include symbolism and figurative language.
- From Dickinson's perspective (using evidence from the poem), would she agree or disagree with the following statements? Explain your answers in writing or in a mock interview with a partner.
  - It is best to know the truth.
  - Truth brings a person to freedom.
  - Truth is reality.
  - Ignorance is bliss.

- Reflect on how this poem relates to another lesson in this unit (e.g., Plato's Allegory, "The Lottery," "The Necklace," McDonaldization, propaganda, Columbus). Develop your own choice of a creative product to show the application of this poem toward another subject studied in this unit. The product may be a chart, skit, interview, piece of art, song, etc. The product should demonstrate how ideas from this lesson converge with an idea from a previous lesson. Write an explanation of how specific lines of the poem relate to concepts within another lesson.

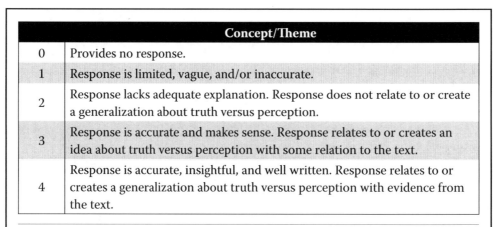

	Concept/Theme
0	Provides no response.
1	Response is limited, vague, and/or inaccurate.
2	Response lacks adequate explanation. Response does not relate to or create a generalization about truth versus perception.
3	Response is accurate and makes sense. Response relates to or creates an idea about truth versus perception with some relation to the text.
4	Response is accurate, insightful, and well written. Response relates to or creates a generalization about truth versus perception with evidence from the text.

Figure 11.2. Scoring guidelines for Lesson 11 formative assessment.

ELA Practice Task

Assign the following task as a performance-based assessment for this lesson: *Is it best to know the truth? In an expository essay, explain how the message of Dickinson's poem "Tell all the truth but tell it slant" addresses the question. Use specific evidence from the poem to develop your response.*

Formative Assessment

1. Ask students to respond to the following prompt in a single paragraph: *What does this poem reveal about truth versus perception?*
2. Use the scoring guidelines in Figure 11.2 to evaluate students' assessments.

Name: _____ Date: _____

Handout 11.1

Blank Literary Analysis Wheel

Directions: Draw arrows across elements to show connections.

Text: _____

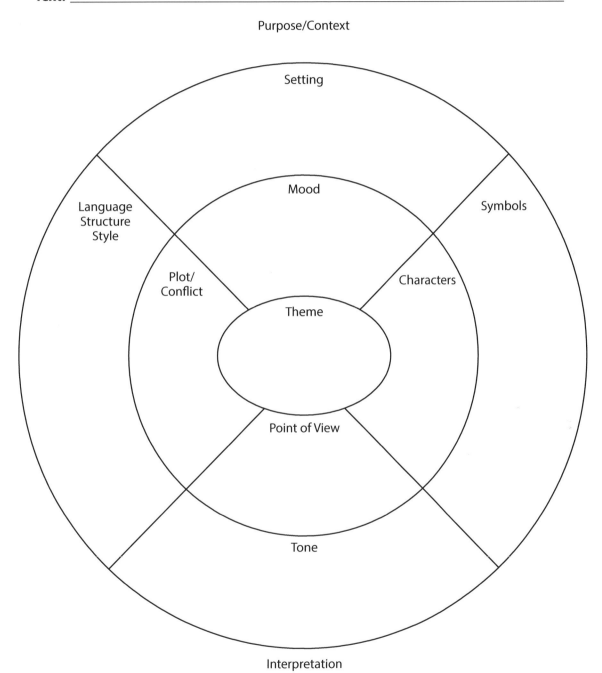

Purpose/Context

Setting

Language Structure Style

Mood

Symbols

Plot/ Conflict

Characters

Theme

Point of View

Tone

Interpretation

Created by Tamra Stambaugh, Ph.D., & Emily Mofield, Ed.D., 2015.

Name: _____ Date: _____

Handout 11.2
Big Idea Reflection

<table>
<tr><td rowspan="3">What?</td><td>Concepts:
What concepts/ideas are in the text?</td><td></td></tr>
<tr><td>Generalizations:
What broad statement can you make about one or more of these concepts? Make it generalizable beyond the text.</td><td></td></tr>
<tr><td>Issue:
What is the main issue, problem, or conflict?</td><td></td></tr>
<tr><td rowspan="2">So What?</td><td>Insight:
What insight on life is provided from this text?</td><td></td></tr>
<tr><td>World/Community/Individual:
How does this text relate to you, your community, or your world? What question does the author want you to ask yourself?</td><td></td></tr>
<tr><td>Now What?</td><td>Implications:
How should you respond to the ideas in the text? What action should you take? What are the implications of the text? What can you do with this information?</td><td></td></tr>
</table>

Created by Emily Mofield, Ed.D., & Tamra Stambaugh, Ph.D., 2015.

CONCLUSION

Lesson

12

Final Reflection and Culminating Project

Goals/Objectives

Content: To analyze and interpret literature, art, and media, students will be able to:

- evaluate how literary or visual elements impact a work's overall message,
- explain with evidence how a writer supports a claim,
- respond to interpretations of texts through a variety of contexts by justifying ideas and providing new information,
- analyze how an individual's motivation and behavior are revealed, and
- relate interpretations of texts to the real world.

Process: To develop thinking, reasoning, and communication skills, students will be able to:

- analyze meaning, purpose, and literary/visual elements;
- make inferences from provided evidence;
- reason through an issue (points of view, assumptions, implications);
- communicate to create, express, and interpret ideas; and
- analyze primary sources (purpose, assumptions, consequences).

Concept: To understand the concept of truth in the language arts, students will be able to:

- make and defend generalizations about truth versus perception,
- explain the positives and negatives of knowing the truth,
- analyze the consequences of believing perception rather than truth, and
- explain the relationship between truth and other concepts.

Materials

- Handout 12.1: *In the Mind's Eye* Culminating Project
- Student may need copies of Blank Literary Analysis Wheel, Big Idea Reflection, Blank Rhetorical Analysis Wheel, Blank Visual Analysis Wheel,

Reasoning About a Situation or Event, and/or Handout 2.3: Concept Organizer, depending on the project they choose (see Appendix B for models)

▪ Rubric 5: Culminating Project Rubric (Appendix C)

Discussion

1. Remind students about the concepts explored in this unit.
   - ▪ Perception of truth varies.
   - ▪ There are positives and negatives in realizing truth.
   - ▪ There are consequences to believing perception rather than truth.

2. Students should review their concept organizers from previous lessons. Ask: *What patterns do you notice? Do you see any similarities? What are the major contrasts? Can you make any other generalizations about truth versus perception based on the unit studied? What evidence is there to support those generalizations?*

Student Independent Reflection

1. Assign the student reflections on Handout 12.1: *In the Mind's Eye* Culminating Project (you may choose to assign all of them or part of them).
2. Guide students through a discussion, reflecting on the unit. Ask: *What blinds one from the truth?* Figure 12.1 provides some sample responses.

Choice-Based Differentiated Products

Assign the culminating project (see Handout 12.1). At teacher discretion, students can present parts of their projects to the class. Use Rubric 5: Culminating Project Rubric to assess student products and applied learning.

Culminating ELA Practice Task

Assign the following task as a culminating performance-based assessment: *What blinds one from realizing truth? After reading several texts, art, and media in this unit, answer the question in a well-developed essay. Refer to at least four works from the unit with textual evidence within your essay.*

Text/Art	What blinds one from the truth?
Relativity by M. C. Escher	Not acknowledging/seeing others' perspectives
"Allegory of the Cave" by Plato	Being content in ignorance; experiencing only the cave for their entire lives
"The Lottery" by Shirley Jackson	Following tradition without question
Starry Night by Vincent Van Gogh	Contrasting emotions; not being valued for uniqueness
Columbus's logs	Superior culture; Eurocentric thinking
Flowers for Algernon by Daniel Keyes	Intellectual IQ and lack of emotional intelligence
"The Necklace" by Guy de Maupassant	Self-centered interest and pride
Propaganda	Governmental persuasive techniques
Fahrenheit 451 by Ray Bradbury	Indifference, apathy
The McDonaldization of Society by George Ritzer	A system that seems rational and functional (but really isn't)
"Tell all the truth but tell it slant" by Emily Dickinson	The whole truth given too fast

Figure 12.1. *What blinds one from the truth?* Sample responses.

Name: _____ Date: _____

Handout 12.1
In the Mind's Eye Culminating Project

STUDENT REFLECTION

Directions: What other movies, stories, historical events, or current events involve these concepts explored in *In the Mind's Eye*? Explain how one story or event demonstrates each concept.

1. Text/Event: _____
   Perception of truth varies.

2. Text/Event: _____
   There are positive and negatives in realizing truth.

3. Text/Event: _____
   There are consequences to believing perception rather than truth.

Name: _____ Date: _____

4. In your own life, how does the theme of truth versus perception manifest itself? How does this unit relate to you personally?

5. Complete the chart to show how each text/art studied answers the question: *What blinds one from truth?*

Text/Art	What blinds one from truth?

Handout 12.1, Continued

Text/Art	What blinds one from truth?

CULMINATING PROJECT

Directions: Choose one activity to demonstrate your understanding of the content, processes, and concepts presented in this unit:

1. Create your own short story that uses the truth versus perception theme. Complete a literary analysis using the Blank Literary Analysis Wheel for your own story. Also

provide concept support by completing Handout 2.3: Concept Organizer for the theme of truth versus perception. Turn in your story, Literary Analysis Wheel, and concept organizer. Include development of dialogue, point of view, setting, plot elements, characterization, symbols, and theme within your story.

2. Study three pieces of visual art that you think relate to the theme of truth versus perception in some way. Complete a visual analysis on each piece. Then, create a three-way Venn diagram on the pieces. Explain in a paragraph or two how each piece exemplifies the theme of truth versus perception. Show the pieces of art to the class and explain the themes to your classmates.

3. Find a primary source that relates to the lives of two individuals introduced in this unit: M. C. Escher, Vincent Van Gogh, Ray Bradbury, Daniel Keyes, Christopher Columbus, Shirley Jackson, George Ritzer, etc. (letters, diaries, autobiographies, interviews, essays they have written). Biographies or information written about them on the Internet are not primary sources. Then, using additional information from secondary sources, determine what is similar between the two individuals. In what ways is the truth versus perception theme evidenced in each of their life experiences? Explain in a couple of paragraphs and include a list of your sources.

4. Using Reasoning About a Situation or Event, evaluate "Does truth bring freedom?" as the situation. Choose four individuals from the unit (characters or real people). Complete the chart: Reasoning About a Situation or Event. Then, create a visual collage or multimedia movie to answer the question "Does truth bring freedom?" Incorporate abstract symbols, words, pictures, and quotes about reality, truth, disillusionment, and/or freedom. Also turn in a written description of symbols used. Refer to Rubric 3: Collage Rubric for specific expectations.

5. Consider real-life applications of the lessons presented (treatment of people with disabilities, misrepresentation of groups of people, the deception of media, negative effects of the McDonaldization of society, negative effects of materialism, and other concepts related to disillusionment or deception). Develop a community service project related to addressing a problem that surfaced within this unit. Complete Reasoning About a Situation or Event concerning the stakeholders involved in the issue. Develop a proposal for an action plan to address the issue as a community service project. Present your proposal to the class in a presentation.

Culminating ELA Practice Task

What blinds one from realizing the truth? After reading several texts, art, and media in this unit, answer the question in a well-developed essay. Refer to at least four works from the unit with textual evidence within your essay.

Posttest
"The Stag and the Pool" *by Aesop*

Directions: Read the text and write your responses to the questions below citing evidence from the text. After reading, complete the questions within 30 minutes on a separate sheet of paper.

A stag saw his shadow reflected in the water, and greatly admired the size of his horns, but felt angry with himself for having such weak feet. While he was thus contemplating himself, a Lion appeared at the pool. The Stag betook himself to flight, and kept himself with ease at a safe distance from the Lion, until he entered a wood and became entangled with his horns. The Lion quickly came up with him and caught him. When too late he thus reproached himself: "Woe is me! How have I deceived myself! These feet which would have saved me I despised, and I gloried in these antlers which have proved my destruction."

1. How does the author's use of literary techniques (e.g., point of view, conflict, plot, language, symbolism, characterization, setting, etc.) contribute to the overall meaning of the passage?

2. "Woe is me! How have I deceived myself! These feet which would have saved me I despised . . . . " What inferences can be made about the stag's motivation and conflict?

3. What does this story suggest about truth versus perception?

Posttest Rubric

"The Stag and the Pool" *by Aesop*

	0	1	2	3	4
Question 1: Content: Literary Analysis	Provides no response.	Response is limited and vague. There is no connection to how literary elements contribute to the meaning, main idea, or theme. A literary element is merely named.	Response is accurate with 1–2 literary techniques described with vague or no connection to a main idea or theme. Response includes limited or no evidence from text.	Response is appropriate and accurate, describing at least two literary elements and a main idea or theme. Response is literal and includes some evidence from the text.	Response is insightful and well supported, describing at least two literary elements and the theme. Response includes abstract connections and substantial evidence from the text.
Question 2: Inference From Evidence	Provides no response.	Response is limited, vague, and/or inaccurate. There is no justification for the answers given.	Response is accurate, but lacks adequate explanation. Response includes some justification for either the character's motivation or conflict.	Response is accurate and makes sense. Response includes some justification about the character's motivation and conflict.	Response is accurate, insightful, interpretive, and well written. Response includes thoughtful justification about the character's motivation and conflict.
Question 3: Concept/ Theme	Provides no response.	Response is limited, vague, and/or inaccurate.	Response lacks adequate explanation. Response does not relate to or create a generalization about truth versus perception. Little or no evidence from text.	Response is accurate and makes sense. Response relates to or creates an idea about truth versus perception with some relation to the text.	Response is accurate, insightful, and well written. Response relates to or creates a generalization about truth versus perception with evidence from the text.

Note: Adapted from *Jacob's Ladder Reading Comprehension Program: Level 4* (p. 148) by T. Stambaugh & J. VanTassel-Baska, 2001, Waco, TX: Prufrock Press. Copyright 2001 by Prufrock Press. Adapted with permission.

References

Assouline, S., Colangelo, N., VanTassel-Baska, J., & Lupkowski-Shoplik, A. (2015). (Eds), *A nation empowered: Evidence trumps the excuses holding back America's brightest students.* Iowa City: University of Iowa, The Connie Belin & Jacqueline N. Blank International Center for Gifted Education and Talent Development.

Bigelow, B. (1992). *Discovering Columbus: Re-reading the past.* Retrieved from http://urbanhabitat.org/node/960

Center for Gifted Education. (n.d.). Reasoning about a situation or event. *Teaching Models.* Retrieved from http://education.wm.edu/centers/cfge/curriculum/teachingmodels

Colangelo, N., Assouline, S., & Gross, M. U. M. (2004). *A nation deceived: How schools hold back America's brightest students* (Vol. II.). Iowa City: University of Iowa, The Connie Belin & Jacqueline N. Blank International Center for Gifted Education and Talent Development.

Flint, V. (n.d.). *The imaginative landscape of Christopher Columbus.* University of Hull, England. Retrieved from http://history-world.org/christopher_columbus.htm

Kulik, J. A., & Kulik, C.-L. C. (1992). Meta-analytic findings on grouping programs. *Gifted Child Quarterly, 36,* 73–77.

Morris, S. B., & DeShon, R. P. (2002). Combining effect size estimates in meta-analysis with repeated measures and independent-groups designs. *Psychological Methods, 7,* 105–125.

Rogers, K. B. (2007). Lessons learned about educating the gifted and talented: A synthesis of the research on educational practice. *Gifted Child Quarterly, 51,* 382–396.

Stambaugh, T., & VanTassel-Baska, J. (2001). *Jacob's ladder reading comprehension program: Level 4.* Waco, TX: Prufrock Press.

Steenberger-Hu, S., & Moon, S. M. (2011). The effects of acceleration on high-ability learners: A meta-analysis. *Gifted Child Quarterly, 55,* 39–53.

VanTassel-Baska, J. (1986). Effective curriculum and instruction models for talented students. *Gifted Child Quarterly,* 30, 164–169.

VanTassel-Baska, J., & Stambaugh, T. (2008). *What works: 20 years of curriculum research and development for high-ability learners.* Center for Gifted Education, College of William and Mary. Waco, TX: Prufrock Press.

Appendix A

Instructions for Using the Models

LITERARY ANALYSIS WHEEL INSTRUCTIONS

The Literary Analysis Model is used to guide students through analyzing how an author uses literary techniques to develop meaning within a work. The model allows students to see connections between multiple literary elements (e.g., setting impacts conflict, conflict reveals character motives and values, characterization impacts theme, etc.).

Using the Literary Analysis Wheel

The Literary Analysis Wheel can be used to guide students through an analysis of a short story, poem, or novel. First, guide students to identify elements of the wheel separately, then emphasize a deeper analysis by asking how elements relate to each other (e.g., point of view impacts theme, setting creates mood, etc.).

The Literary Analysis Wheel is meant to be interactive. The inner wheel conceptually spins so that its elements interact with each other and the outer wheel. Each element can relate to each other, regardless of its placement on the wheel.

The Literary Analysis Wheel Guide (Appendix B) shows specific prompts for each element of the wheel. The teacher may simply refer to the model during instruction or students may take notes on the Blank Literary Analysis Wheel using arrows to show how the various elements relate. It is suggested that students note the answers to the "simple" questions on the graphic organizer, and then discuss interactions with other elements. Consider making a poster of the Literary Analysis Wheel Guide and posting it in your classroom for students to refer to throughout the unit.

Once students are accustomed to using the wheel, encourage students to develop their own questions about the relationship between elements.

Students can make their own interactive paper-plate model of the wheel. Two different colored papers may be used for the inner and outer circles, secured with a brass paper fastener. Students may use the wheels as visuals in small groups.

178 **Sample questions for literary analysis.** The following questions can be asked to support students in analyzing literature. Note that complexity is added by combining elements.

- **Simple:**
  - **Character:** *What are the values and motives of the characters? What evidence supports this? How does the author reveal character?*
  - **Setting:** *What is the time and place of the story?*
  - **Tone:** *What is the author's attitude toward the subject? With what attitude does the author approach the theme?*
  - **Symbols:** *How do objects or names represent more abstract ideas?*
  - **Point of View:** *What is the narrator's point of view (first person, third person objective, third person limited, third person omniscient)?*
  - **Language/Style/Structure:** *What figurative language and imagery does the author use? What is the author's style?*
  - **Plot/Conflict:** *What are the significant internal and external conflicts of the story? What are the significant parts of the plot?*
  - **Mood:** *What is the feeling the reader gets from the story? How is this established?*
  - **Theme:** *What is the author's main message that can be generalized to broader contexts? (The theme is the author's point of view on a given subject.)*

- **Complex:**
  - Setting+
    - *How does the setting influence the development of the theme?*
    - *How does the setting affect the mood?*
    - *What language does the author use to describe the setting (e.g., use of imagery, similes, etc.)?*
    - *How does the setting enhance conflict? How does the setting provoke plot events?*
    - *How is the setting symbolic of a larger idea (e.g., autumn, twilight)?*
    - *How does the setting affect and change the characters?*
    - *How does the setting help reveal the author's tone/attitude toward the theme/subject?*
    - *What conflicts could only happen in this setting? How does this influence the plot and theme?*

  - Symbols+
    - *How do symbols help develop the theme?*
    - *How does the author use figurative language to establish symbolism?*
    - *How do symbols relate to key plot elements and conflicts?*

- *How do symbols contribute to establishing the mood?*
- *Is the setting symbolic of a larger idea (e.g., twilight, autumn)?*
- *How does the author's use of symbols reveal the author's tone?*
- *How are characters symbolic of archetypes? What symbols are associated with the characters?*

- Character+
  - *How do the characters' actions/beliefs/attitudes/struggles influence the theme?*
  - *How do the qualities of the characters affect the conflict as it relates to significant parts of the plot?*
  - *How do the characters' actions and responses establish mood?*
  - *What characters' thoughts/feelings are hidden and/or revealed by the narrator's point of view? How does this impact the reader's experience of the story?*
  - *How does the author use language to develop character? Consider dialect, descriptions, use of figurative language, and names.*
  - *Are characters revealed by symbols?*
  - *How does the setting affect character actions?*
  - *How does the author's tone toward the subject influence the development of characters?*

- Tone+
  - *How does the author's tone help establish the theme? What attitude does the author take in approaching the theme?*
  - *How is the author's tone revealed in the narrator's point of view (e.g., the narrator's words and feelings will reveal the attitude of how the author approaches the theme)?*
  - *What words/phrases does the author use to establish tone? How does the tone change throughout the story? How is this established through the author's style?*
  - *How is the author's tone revealed in the plot and conflicts? What specific textual evidence supports this?*
  - *How do the characters' conflicts reveal the author's tone toward a subject?*
  - *How does the author's tone aid in developing the mood of the story?*
  - *How do symbols help reveal the author's tone?*
  - *How do character actions, values, and conflicts reveal the author's tone?*
  - *How does the setting help reveal the author's tone/attitude toward the subject?*

- Point of View+
  - *How does the narrator's point of view shape the theme?*
  - *How does the narrator's point of view establish mood (e.g., the reader depends on the narrator's perspective in telling the story, so the reader feels the way the narrator does about what is being described)?*
  - *How does the narrator's point of view affect the way the reader views the significant conflicts and plot events?*
  - *What is the style of the narrator? How does the narrator's point of view (specifically, voice and diction) affect the story?*
  - *How is the author's tone revealed in the narrator's point of view (e.g., the narrator's words and feelings will reveal the attitude of how the author approaches the theme)?*
  - *What character thoughts are revealed or hidden because of the narrator's point of view? How does this impact the reader's experience of the story?*

- Language/Style/Structure+
  - *How does the author's use of figurative language or imagery contribute to literary elements?*
  - *How does the dialect of the characters contribute to our understanding of literary elements?*
  - *How does the author's style and sentence structure enhance the mood?*

- Mood+
  - *How does the mood help develop the theme? What if the mood were different, how would this change the theme of the story?*
  - *How does the author's point of view help create mood?*
  - *How does the author's tone create mood for the reader?*
  - *How do the character's actions, thoughts, and conflicts contribute to the mood?*
  - *How does the setting contribute to the mood?*
  - *How does the author use specific language to develop the mood?*
  - *How do specific symbols help establish the mood?*

- Plot/Conflict+
  - *How does the plot develop the theme? How would the theme be different if the story had a different ending?*
  - *How does the conflict reveal the character's values and motives?*
  - *How does setting impact the conflict and plot?*

- *What insight about the conflict does the reader have (or not have) as a result of the narrator's point of view?*
- *How do symbols represent aspects of the conflict (also consider fore-shadowing devices)?*
- *How do character actions, thoughts, and conflicts reveal the author's tone?*
- *How does the plot and conflict reveal and/or change the mood?*
- *How does the author's style contribute to the development of the plot? Why does the author use more language/description on certain aspects of the plot than others?*

- Theme+
  - *How does the plot impact the theme? How would the theme change if key parts of the plot or ending were changed?*
  - *How does the theme impact the development of the plot? If the author wanted to show a different theme, how would he have to change the plot of the story? How would the characters' values, motives, and actions change?*
  - *How do the literary elements contribute to the development of the theme?*

- **Interpretation:**
  - *Taken altogether, what is your interpretation of the work (e.g., what is the explanation or meaning of this work given the author's use of various literary elements)? How did literary elements combine to create meaning? Support your interpretation by referring to the interaction of multiple elements in shaping your understanding of the work.*

Example Literary Analysis Lesson

Read the poem "I like to see it lap the Miles" by Emily Dickinson available at http://www.poets.org/poetsorg/poem/i-see-it-lap-miles-43.

Step 1: Text-dependent questions. Lead students through a close reading of text. (*Note:* Do not give away that the poem is about a train; students should continue to hypothesize and discuss with textual evidence).

- According to the poem, does the author enjoy watching this object? How do you know? (Sample response: Yes, the first line of the poem states, "I like to see it . . . ")
- According to the poem, does the author like the object itself? How do you know? (Sample response: No, negative connotations about the object—supercilious, complaining, horrid, hooting—are combined with its omnip-

otence. It carves out the quarry to fit its own needs, to "fit its sides"—which is not welcomed in Dickinson's world.)

- What feelings can we associate with some of the words in this poem (horrid, hooting, omnipotent, supercilious, complaining, docile, punctual)? Are the connotations positive or negative?

- How do these connotations change and what effect does it have on the poem? (Sample response: They change from negative to positive.)

- After a second reading, students should respond to a partner: What is this poem about? (Most may say a horse, but help students understand that it is being compared to a horse, continue to guide them as they "discover" it is a railway train.) What evidence is there to support your idea? (The poem is about a train that is compared to a horse. Ask students to highlight or underline all comparisons of the train symbolized through a horse. Note that a train was referred to as an "iron horse" during the time period.)

Step 2. Literary Analysis Wheel, separate elements. Lead students through a simple analysis by completing the separate parts of the wheel.

- **Setting:** What is the setting? What words are used to describe the setting?

- **Character:** Considering the train as a character, what are the train's values and motives? (Sample response: The train is the "iron horse," which is proud and powerful, changing the landscape to fit its own needs. The train's values are to be efficient and strong, with a motivation to arrive punctually at its destination.)

- **Point of View:** What is Dickinson's point of view toward the object? How do you know? (Sample response: She sees both the negative and positive qualities.) (*Note:* Because this is a poem, we are considering the author's point of view—however, in short stories and novels, consider first person, third limited, omniscient, and objective point of view.)

- **Language:** Do you notice any specific figurative language or sound devices throughout the poem? (Sample response: Alliteration: "like," "lap," "lick;" "stop," "step;" personification: "lick," "stop," "feed itself;" simile: "neigh like Boangeres;" rhythm: unaccented-accented syllable pattern.)

- **Symbol:** What does the horse imagery represent? Why is the symbol of a horse used? How is the allusion to Boangeres a symbol? (Sample response: The horse is a symbol for the iron horse—a train. Boangeres was a vociferous disciple—loud and annoying—symbolic of the train.)

- **Tone:** What is Dickinson's attitude toward the train? What is the tone? (Sample response: Her tone is ambiguous—it is both positive and negative—she hates it but is also in awe of its power. At times her tone can also be unwelcoming and unapproving. Note how this is affected by her point of view and language.)

- **Conflict:** What is the significant conflict in the poem? (Sample response: Technology vs. nature.)
- **Theme:** What is the author's main message? (Sample response: Themes may relate to the the power of change, power of technology, or the intrusion of technology on nature.)
- **Mood:** Since this is a poem, it would be a stretch to be able to describe the mood based on the few lines that are given. It is suggested that this is not part of the poem analysis.

Step 3. Combined elements for complexity. Discuss how multiple elements interact to establish an overall interpretation of the poem.

- *How does Dickinson's use of language help develop our understanding of the character and the narrator's point of view?* She uses both positive ("docile," "omnipotent") and negative ("horrid," "Boangeres," "supercilious") connotations to show an ambiguous point of view—she loves and hates the train at the same time. The positive and negative connotations about the character help establish Dickinson's point of view.
- *How does the use of language help develop symbolism?* The horse imagery ("neigh," "feed itself at tanks," "stable") establishes the idea of "the iron horse." The *st-* alliteration helps create the sound a horse might make. The rhythm of the poem almost sounds like a train. The entire poem is a metaphor (horse compared to train) and supported through similes (e.g., "neigh like Boangeres") and personification ("lick the valleys," "feed itself," "step").
- *How does setting help establish our understanding of the train's character? How does the setting help us understand the conflict?* The train can be considered as the main character, the "iron horse," who is proud and powerful, changing the landscape to fit its own needs. It pares a quarry to meet its own needs. The use of "shanties" in the setting implies how the train condescendingly looks down upon human things. The train "licks" the valleys up, revealing how it authoritatively takes layers off the landscape.
- *How does the tone and conflict establish the theme of the poem?* Dickinson's tone and attitude toward the new technology establishes the conflict of nature versus technology. This clearly establishes the theme of the power and intrusion of technology on our lives.
- *If Dickinson were to change the theme to "overcoming obstacles," how would this affect how she describes the setting and character?* The character (the train) would be described more positively or even heroic. The setting would not showcase the train's domination; rather, it might be a hindrance to a train. Consider how the story "The Little Engine That Could" shows a contrasting theme (e.g., the setting poses an obstacle for the train instead of

the train imposing on nature; rather than the train having "power" over the setting, the setting poses "power" over the train).

VISUAL ANALYSIS WHEEL INSTRUCTIONS

The Visual Analysis Model is used to guide students through analyzing how an artist develops a main idea in art. Students analyze specific techniques, organization, and the artist's point of view toward the idea. Additionally, students examine prominent images and symbolism, the author's background, and emotions portrayed and evoked in the art. The model allows students to see the connection between multiple concepts (e.g., images are organized intentionally to create the main idea, point of view is influenced by the artist's background, specific techniques are used to evoke emotion, etc.).

Using the Visual Analysis Wheel

The Visual Analysis Wheel can be used to guide students through an in-depth analysis of art or visual media. It is meant to be interactive. The inner circle conceptually spins so that it interacts with elements on the outer circle.

The Visual Analysis Wheel Guide (Appendix B) shows specific prompts to guide students in thinking through each separate element. The teacher may simply refer to the model during instruction or students may take notes on the Blank Visual Analysis Wheel using arrows to show how the elements relate. It is suggested that students first note the answers to each concept separately on the graphic organizer, and then discuss how they influence each other.

Students can make their own interactive paper-plate model of the wheel. Two different colored papers may be used for the inner and outer circles, secured with a brass paper fastener. Students may use the wheels as visuals in small groups.

Sample questions for visual analysis. The following questions can be asked for analyzing art. Note that complexity is added by combining different elements.

- **Purpose:**
  - *What is the purpose of the art?*

- **Context:**
  - *What year was this art created? What artistic movements may have influenced this work? What type of art is this? What historical events are happening at the time this was made? Is there a specific audience for which the art was created?*

- **Main Idea/Message:**
  - *What is the main idea of this art? What is the message of the art?*

- **Techniques:**
  - *What specific techniques does the artist use? (Consider color, shape, brushstroke, patterns, contrast.)*

- **Point of View/Assumptions:**
  - *What is the artist's point of view toward the topic?*
  - *What assumptions does the artist make?*
  - *What is the artist's unstated premise or belief? What does the artist take for granted about the audience?*

- **Structure:**
  - *How does the artist organize ideas?*
  - *What is the central part of the painting?*
  - *Where is your eye drawn first? Why?*

- **Images/Symbols:**
  - *What are the main images?*
  - *Do they symbolize a deeper meaning? How?*

- **Images/Structure:**
  - *Why does the artist intentionally place the objects where they are?*

- **Images/Point of View/Assumptions:**
  - *What do the artist's images reveal about his or her point of view/assumptions about the topic displayed?*

- **Images/Techniques:**
  - *What specific techniques does the artist use to create the main images of the art?*

- **Images/Purpose/Context:**
  - *How does the historical context influence the artist's choice of images in his art?*
  - *How does the audience for which this is intended influence the artist's choice of images?*

- **Emotions:**
  - *What emotions does this art evoke in you?*
  - *What emotions does this art reveal/portray?*

- **Emotions/Point of View/Assumptions:**
  - *How does the artist's point of view toward the topic influence your emotional reaction to the art?*

- **Emotions/Technique:**
  - *What techniques does the artist use to portray and evoke emotion from his or her art?*

- **Emotions/Structure:**
  - *Are parts of the art more emotionally powerful than others? How did the artist organize his or her painting to evoke or portray emotion?*

- **Emotions/Purpose/Context:**
  - *How does the historical situation influence how the artist expresses or evokes emotion?*

- **Artist Background:**
  - *What do you know about the artist's personal life? Who influenced his or her work? How did his or her work influence others?*

- **Artist Background/Technique:**
  - *What techniques does the artist use that are unique to his or her style?*

- **Artist Background/Point of View/Assumptions:**
  - *How does the artist's background influence his or her point of view/ assumptions about the topic?*

- **Artist Background/Structure:**
  - *Does the artist's background influence the way he or she organizes his or her art?*

- **Artist Background/Purpose/Context:**
  - *How is the artist influenced by the historical context of his or her time? How does the artist influence the historical context of his or her time?*

- **Implications:**
  - *What are the short- and long-term consequences of this art?*
  - *What are the implications for you after viewing this art?*

- **Evaluation:**
  - *Do you like this art? Why or why not? Use specific elements for the wheel in your answer.*
  - *What does this art make you think? Would you hang this in your home? Why or why not?*
  - *What elements of this art are most important to consider and why?*

Example Visual Analysis Lesson

Students view the lithograph "Relativity" by M. C. Escher (available online). Do not reveal the title.

Step 1: Close viewing questions. Lead students through an initial viewing of the art.

- What detail of this art is interesting to you? (Ask every student; short response.)
- How many staircases are there? (Sample response: Seven; some overlap.)
- How many sources of gravity are in this picture? (Sample response: Three.)
- What behaviors do you see of the people?
- What is the focal point of the picture? Justify your answer.
- How does Escher produce "dual effects" within this art? (Sample response: The ceiling is also a floor.) Note that although two people may be on the same staircase, they exist in two separate dimensions. Do they know of each other's existence? (Sample response: One is going up, one is going down, but they are going in the same direction.)
- Round-robin: If you had to give the lithograph a title, what title would you give it? (Ask every student; short response.)
- Share with your neighbor why you chose this title (or if time permits, elicit this as whole group).
- Share the real title of the lithograph. "Relativity." Why do you think Escher gave it this title?

Step 2. Visual Analysis Wheel, separate elements. Lead students through completing relevant parts of the Visual Analysis Wheel during discussion. Focus first on the separate elements.

- **Purpose/Context:**
  - *What is the context of this art?* Lithograph printed in 1953.
  - *What do you think his purpose/motive is in creating this?* To express an idea of reality. (*Note:* Students may not be able to determine this until after discussing the art to some extent.)

188

Point of View/Assumptions:

- *What is Escher's point of view toward reality?* Escher is revealing that there are multiple experiences and perceptions of reality. People perceive reality differently.

Images:

- *What do you believe are the most prominent images in the picture? Why? How might they be symbols for something deeper?* Staircases = journey in life; featureless people = unaware people, emotionless; windows to outside = ways to get out of isolation.

Emotions:

- *What emotions does this evoke in you? What emotions are revealed?* The featureless people reveal a lack of emotion, indicating that people are coming and going in life in an emotionless state.

Artist Background:

- *What do you know about the artist's background? How is the artist influenced by the historical context of his time?* M. C. Escher (1898–1972) was a famous 20th-century Dutch artist who is known for developing impossible structures within his art. He made more than 448 lithographs (original prints) and woodcarvings, and more than 2,000 drawings. Escher also wrote many poems and essays, and he studied architecture, although he never graduated from high school. He used many mathematical aspects in his works. Most of Escher's works involve his own fascination with the concept of reality. His works showing paradoxes, tessellations, and impossible objects have had influence on graphic art, psychology, philosophy, and logic.

Main Idea:

- *What is Escher conveying about life in this painting? What is Escher's main idea?* Truth/reality is relative; each person has his or her own perception of reality and may be unaware of others' realities.

Implications:

- *What are the implications of this art on you the viewer?*

- **Evaluation:**
  - *Do you like this art? Would you hang it in your home? Does it make you think? Was the artist successful in presenting his ideas? Justify your answers with evidence.*

Step 3. Combined elements for complexity. Combine elements to develop more complex questions. Students may draw arrows on their wheels to show how elements relate (images + techniques, etc.).

- **Images/Technique:**
  - *What techniques does Escher use to enhance images?* The people are all identical and featureless. There are three sources of gravity and six staircases. The outside world is park-like. Some appear to be climbing upside down, but according to their gravity, they are climbing the staircase normally. Parts of the picture look two-dimensional, other parts look three-dimensional. He includes paradoxes (two people standing on same staircase in separate realities). The basements add a surreal effect.

- **Images/Structure:**
  - *How does Escher intentionally place the objects in the drawing to reveal meaning?* He purposefully draws two people standing on the same step (top center); they coexist yet they are in different gravity worlds. *What does this reveal about life?* We are preoccupied with our own journeys, we do not acknowledge others' points of view.

- **Artist Background/Technique:**
  - *What techniques does Escher use that are unique to his style?* Escher creates impossible realities within this work (three gravity worlds existing as one). He is known for creating paradoxes in his art.

- **Emotions/Structure/Technique:**
  - *How did the artist organize his art to portray or evoke emotion? What techniques were used to evoke or portray emotion?* It is interesting that the staircase structure is an upside-down triangle. Perhaps this is to give a more chaotic feel to the picture. Those within the staircases are "lost" in a world of coming and going, living life unaware beyond their own self-centered world. His technique of painting featureless people portrays a lack of emotion. The lack of emotion interplays with a main idea that the people are not aware of each other's existence, particularly in the other gravity worlds.

RHETORICAL ANALYSIS WHEEL INSTRUCTIONS

The Rhetorical Analysis Model is used to analyze how an author develops and supports an argument. Students examine how a writer achieves his or her purpose by analyzing how several elements work together to create an effective argument. This includes thinking about the rhetorical situation (e.g., purpose, context, audience), means of persuasion (e.g., ethos, logos, and pathos appeals), and rhetorical strategies (e.g., techniques, evidence, structure, etc.). The author develops a claim through the use of three rhetorical appeals: logos (reasoning), pathos (emotion), and ethos (credibility) in response to the situation. These rhetorical appeals are developed by point of view, specific strategies, techniques, and organization. The model allows students to see connections between multiple elements (e.g., credibility is influenced by point of view, specific techniques are used to evoke emotion, structure develops strong logos appeals, etc.).

Overview of Aristotle's Rhetorical Appeals

Aristotle's rhetoric includes logos, ethos, and pathos appeals. This enhances a writer's ability to persuade an audience.

- **Logos:** How the author establishes good reasoning to make his message make sense. This includes major points, use of evidence, syllogisms, examples, evidence, facts, statistics, etc. Text focused.
- **Pathos:** How the author appeals to the audience's emotion. Audience focused.
- **Ethos:** How the author develops credibility and trust. Author focused.

Using the Rhetorical Analysis Wheel

The Rhetorical Analysis Wheel can be used to analyze how an author develops a claim through rhetorical appeals, techniques, and structure. Students also think through the point of view, assumptions, purpose, and implications of the document. It is meant to be interactive. The inner circle conceptually spins so that it interacts with elements on the outer circle.

The Rhetorical Analysis Wheel Guide (Appendix B) shows specific prompts to guide students in thinking through each separate element. The teacher may simply refer to the model during instruction or students may take notes on the Blank Rhetorical Analysis Wheel using arrows to show how elements relate. It is suggested that students first note the answers to each element separately on the graphic organizer, and then discuss how they influence each other. Consider making a poster of the Rhetorical Analysis Wheel Guide to refer to throughout the unit.

Students can make their own interactive paper-plate model of the wheel. Two different colored papers may be used for the inner and outer circles, secured with a brass paper fastener. Students may use the wheels as visuals in small groups.

Sample questions for rhetorical analysis. The following questions can be asked for analyzing argument. Note that complexity is added by combining elements.

- **Purpose:**
  - *What is the author's purpose?*

- **Context/Audience:**
  - *Who is the audience and what is the historical situation?*
  - *What is the main problem in the historical context?*

- **Claim:**
  - *What is the main claim or message of the text?*

- **Techniques:**
  - *What specific techniques does the writer use to develop his or her claim?* Here are some examples of specific techniques that may be used:
    - **Language:** Consider how specific word choice and style develop tone.
    - **Positive and negative connotations of words:** Consider how words evoke feelings.
    - **Personification:** Human qualities given to nonhuman objects/ideas.
    - **Simile:** A figure of speech that compares two unlike things using "like" or "as."
    - **Metaphor:** A direct comparison between two unlike things.
    - **Hyperbole:** An extreme exaggeration.
    - **Allusion:** A reference to a historical or Biblical work, person, or event. The writer assumes the reader can make connections between the allusion and the text being read.
    - **Imagery:** Formation of mental images that appeal to the senses.
    - **Parallelism:** Using similar grammatical structures in order to emphasize related ideas.
    - **Repetition:** Repeating the same wording for emphasis, clarity, or emotional impact.
    - **Contrast:** A striking difference of ideas for effect.
    - **Rhetorical question:** A question asked by the writer, but not expected to be answered aloud. It evokes reflection.
    - **Liberty rhetoric:** Using patriotic appeals for freedom.
    - **War rhetoric:** Reasoning to convince someone that war is necessary.

- ◆ **Syllogism:** A form of deductive logic—a conclusion drawn from two premises. Example: If x=y and y=z, then x=z. If citizens can vote and if women are citizens, then women should be allowed to vote.
- ◆ **Use of evidence, facts, statistics, examples, and counterclaims (strongly connects with logos):** Explicit support for the argument.

■ **Point of View/Assumptions:**
- • *What is the writer's point of view toward the topic?*
- • *What assumptions does the writer make?*
- • *What is the writer's unstated premise or belief? What does the writer take for granted about the audience?*

■ **Structure/Organization:**
- • *How does the writer organize ideas (e.g., problem-solution, point by point, chronologically, sequentially, compare/contrast)?*
- • *Where is the thesis? Why is it here?*
- • *Does the writer structure his message deductively or inductively?*

■ **Logos (Focus on Text):**
- • *What reasoning is used to help the argument make sense? What are the main points?*
- • *Are statements easy to accept or does the writer need to provide more evidence?*
- • *What research, facts, statistics, or expert opinions are used? Are these sufficient?*
- • **Logos/Structure**
    - ◆ *How does the structure of the document help the writer's argument make sense?*

- • **Logos/Point of View:**
    - ◆ *Does the writer assume that the audience already accepts a premise?*
    - ◆ *What do the writer's examples and facts (or lack of) reveal about his or her assumptions about the audience?*

- • **Logos/Techniques:**
    - ◆ *Which techniques are used to help the writer logically form his or her argument (e.g., syllogisms, comparisons, parallelisms, use of statistics, examples, etc.)?*

- **Logos/Context:**
  - *How do the problem, context, and audience influence the writer's approach in developing a logical argument? Because the historical situation is what it is, how does this influence the way the writer organizes his reasoning?*

- **Pathos (Focus on Audience):**
  - *How does the writer appeal to the audience's emotions (guilt, fear, pride, etc.)?*
  - *What word connotations or imagery does the writer use to evoke emotion in the audience?*
  - *How do pathos appeals help the writer establish his claim?*
  - **Pathos/Point of View:**
    - *How does the writer's tone and point of view impact the desired emotional response?*
    - *How does the writer's bias influence the desired emotional response?*

  - **Pathos/Technique:**
    - *What techniques does the writer use to evoke emotion among the audience (e.g., repetition, liberty rhetoric, war rhetoric, similes, hyperbole, symbolism, rhetorical questions)?*

  - **Pathos/Structure:**
    - *Where does the writer place the emotional appeals? Why is this important? Do pathos appeals change throughout the text? How? Why? How does this enhance or take away from the argument?*

  - **Pathos/Context:**
    - *How does the historical situation/problem influence how the writer uses pathos appeals? How do pathos appeals help the writer accomplish his desired effect?*

- **Ethos (Focus on Writer):**
  - *Is the writer credible?*
  - *How does the writer establish trust?*
  - *Are sources credible?*
  - *Does the writer respect an opposing viewpoint?*
  - *Does the writer address counterclaims? How?*
  - *How do ethos appeals help the writer establish an effective argument?*

- **Ethos/Technique:**
  - *What techniques does the writer use to establish credibility (e.g., uses reliable sources, discusses character/reputation, etc.)?*

- **Ethos/Point of View:**
  - *Does the writer's bias take away from his or her credibility?*
  - *Do the writer's assumptions about the opposing point of view reduce his or her credibility?*

- **Ethos/Structure:**
  - *Where in the document does the writer develop his or her credibility? Why is it significant he or she places his or her ethos appeals here?*
  - *Where does the writer address counterclaims? How does he or she address the counterclaim, and how does this enhance or reduce his or her credibility?*

- **Ethos/Context:**
  - *Why is it important for the writer to develop trust with this audience in this historical situation?*
  - *What must the writer consider about the audience when establishing his or her credibility?*

- **Implications:**
  - *What are the short- and long-term implications/consequences of this document?*

- **Evaluation:**
  - *How effective is the writer in developing his or her claim? To what extent is the purpose fulfilled?*
  - *Is there a balance of pathos, ethos, and logos appeals?*
  - *Is there too much bias or emotional manipulation? Is there adequate evidence to support the claim(s)? Is the evidence credible, rational, and organized logically?*

Students should consider the author's purpose (to entertain, inform, persuade, express) when determining how effective the argument is. For example, it may not be necessary to provide counterarguments if the purpose of the text is not to persuade. Students should also consider the balance of logos, ethos, and pathos appeals.

Example Rhetorical Analysis Lesson

Students should read the excerpt from Franklin D. Roosevelt's Second Inaugural Address (see p. 201).

Step 1: Text-dependent questions. Lead students through a close reading of the text for initial comprehension. You may also ask students to paraphrase sections of the text into their own words.

- According to Roosevelt, what brings an ever richer life to Americans?
- Why does Roosevelt personify Comfort, Opportunism, and Timidity? How are these "voices" considered distractions?
- What are some of the positive aspects of the current state of affairs?
- According to the text, why is prosperity dangerous?
- What is meant by "prosperity already tests the persistence of our progressive purpose"?
- Which one of Roosevelt's "I see" statements is most powerful?
- According to the text, how do we test our progress?
- What is Roosevelt's solution to the problems of tens of millions?
- What four words are most important to the text? Can you put these four words together in a sentence to summarize FDR's main message?

Step 2: Teach elements of rhetorical analysis. Teach students some basic principles of a rhetorical analysis:

- **Modes of Rhetoric (Logos, Pathos, Ethos):** Explain Aristotle's modes of rhetoric (see p. 190).
- **Techniques:** Students will consider how these appeals are developed through different techniques used by the author. Go over a few techniques with students (see p. 191). Note that language, positive and negative connotations, personification, repetition, and rhetorical questions are used.
- **Structure/Organization:** Students should consider where the appeals are placed within the documents and why they are there. They should also consider the overall structure of the document as it often supports the logos appeal (it helps the author's rationale "make sense" by putting ideas in this order). Why is it important that the points are placed structurally where they are? Throughout the analysis, the elements of logos, ethos, and pathos interact with structure, techniques and point of view.

Step 3: Rhetorical Analysis Wheel: Separate Elements. Lead students through completing relevant parts of the Rhetorical Analysis Wheel. Students do not need to write detailed explanations on the organizer, just notes. Focus first on the separate elements.

- **Purpose:**
  - *What is Roosevelt's purpose in delivering this message?* To persuade the American people to carry on toward progress by moving forward together.

- **Message/Claim:**
  - *What is Roosevelt's main claim? What is the main idea he is proving?* America will carry on toward progress by addressing concerns of all.

- **Point of View/Assumptions:**
  - *What is Roosevelt's point of view toward progress? What are his assumptions?* FDR believes Americans should cautiously handle prosperity; it can distract Americans from progressing because of the self-interest involved. He assumes that government involvement into the affairs of people is welcomed, justified, and of goodwill.

- **Structure:**
  - *What is the overall structure of the speech?* Problem-solution.

- **Techniques:**
  - *What are some techniques you notice within the speech?* Rhetorical questions, personification, etc.

- **Logos:**
  - *What are the main points? How does the author support his claim with evidence and facts? What are the main "reasons" that support the claim?* **Logos/Reasoning:** FDR notes that America has progressed, but not arrived, and the American people should be warned by the disasters of prosperity. He lists positive state of affairs, lists negative state of affairs, and explains a hopeful future via government involvement. He provides evidence of a negative state of affairs ("I see millions . . . ").

- **Pathos:**
  - *What emotion(s) does the author attempt to evoke in the audience (pathos)?* FDR appeals to a sense of sympathy ("I see millions . . . ") and pride ("If I know aught of the will of our people . . . ").

- **Ethos:**
  - *Is the author credible? How does the author establish trust? Is evidence credible?* FDR is speaking at his second inaugural address and acknowledges the progress made during his presidency. He also refers to the

government as effective and competent to build trust. Evidence is not supported with specific credibility, and he is somewhat biased with his enthusiasm for a competent government addressing problems.

- **Implications:**
  - *What are the short- and long-term implications/consequences of this document?* This speech set the stage for many of FDR's initiatives. During his second term, Congress passed the Housing Act, laws were made to establish minimum wage (Fair Labor Standards Act), and more than 3.3 million jobs were developed through WPA (Works Progress Administration).

Step 4: Combined elements for complexity. Combine elements to develop more complex questions. Students may draw arrows on their wheels to show how elements relate (pathos + techniques, etc.).

- **Logos/Techniques:**
  - *What techniques are used to develop the reasoning in his argument?* He sets up the first point by asking a rhetorical question ("Shall we pause now and turn our back . . . "), uses personification to introduce the idea that we should be warned by the disasters of prosperity ("Comfort says . . . timidity says . . . "), addresses a counterclaim and acknowledges that we have progressed ("true, we have come far . . . "), and explains how progress today is more difficult in light of prosperity.

- **Logos/Structure:**
  - *How is the argument structured logically?* Problem-solution. It is also organized inductively. His main claim is that Americans will carry on by addressing the concerns of all. He provides evidence first and then makes this claim.

- **Pathos/Techniques:**
  - *What techniques are used to develop pathos appeals?* He uses repetition ("I see millions . . . ") to develop sympathy. He develops a sense of urgency with "at this very moment . . . " He uses loaded language ("meager," "indecent," "poverty," "denying work," "ill-housed," "ill-clad," "ill-nourished") for sympathy and pride ("goodwill," "effective government," "uncorrupted by cancers of injustice," "strong," "will to peace," "long-cherished ideals").

- **Pathos/Structure:**
  - *Where does he place pathos appeals (structure)? Why? Do they change? Why?* The pathos appeals are in line with the problem-solution logos structure. As he develops the problem, he evokes sympathy. As he develops the solution, he evokes pride.

- **Ethos/Techniques/Structure:**
  - *What techniques are used to establish ethos appeals and why are they placed where they are?* He includes "we," and "us" throughout the speech to connect with the audience. As he uses "we," he establishes that he has been a part of the present gains. The "we" language shifts to "I"—revealing that the audience can really trust him because he himself sees the problems. He shifts again to "we" when connecting the audience to the goodwill of the nation.

- **Evaluation:**
  - *How effective is the author in supporting his claim? Is there a balance of pathos, ethos, and logos appeals? Is the claim fully supported?* Roosevelt is effective in supporting the claim that America will continue on toward progress by addressing the concerns of all. There is a balance of logos, ethos, and pathos appeals. FDR gives sufficient evidence of the problem with the repeated "I see" statements, although the credibility of this evidence is not specific, but general.

Text Analysis Example, Simplified Version

Some teachers of younger grades may wish to focus on how the author supports a central idea by using relevant and sufficient evidence. This model does not focus on the rhetorical appeals (logos, ethos, and pathos) to support a claim, rather it focuses on why the author chose to use specific points to advance a central idea.

The following are simple and complex questions that could be used:

- **Purpose:**
  - *What is Roosevelt's purpose in delivering this message?* To persuade the American people to carry on toward progress by moving forward together.

- **Central Idea:**
  - *What is FDR's central idea (main message)?* We will carry on toward progress by addressing concerns of all.

■ **Point of View/Assumptions:**
- *What is FDR's point of view toward progress? What are his assumptions?* FDR believes Americans should cautiously handle prosperity; it can distract us from progressing because of the self-interest involved. He assumes that government involvement into the affairs of people is welcomed, justified, and of goodwill.

■ **Point 1/Evidence:**
- *What is one important point FDR makes to develop his central idea?* **Point 1:** We should we warned by the disasters of prosperity. **Evidence:** "Comfort says, 'tarry a while.' Opportunism . . . . To hold progress today, however, is more difficult . . . . "
- *How does this point develop his central idea?* This explains the state of affairs—the nation has made great progress and experienced prosperity, but prosperity can also present a problem. He asks the nation to consider the nature of progress.
- *What techniques are used to develop this point?* He personifies comfort, opportunism, and timidity to explain that the nation is at a place of decision in the face of prosperity. He describes symptoms of prosperity with negative word connotations ("dulled conscience, irresponsibility . . . ").
- *Why is it important the author discusses this point at this particular part of the speech (structure)?* This allows him to introduce the problem of prosperity. This sets him up to explain to the audience that not everyone is reaping the benefits of prosperity, which is important in developing his central idea.

■ **Point 2/Evidence:**
- *What is another important point FDR uses to develop his central idea?* **Point 2:** He explains a negative state of affairs. **Evidence:** "I see millions . . . ill-housed, ill-clad, ill-nourished."
- *How does this point develop the central idea?* It explains the problem of poverty, that the concerns of all citizens are not addressed even within a time of prosperous progress.
- *What techniques are used to develop his point?* He uses both repetition ("I see millions") and loaded language ("meager," "indecent," "poverty," "denying work," "ill-housed," "ill-clad," "ill-nourished") to develop sympathy (pathos appeal).
- *Why is it important that the author discusses this point at this particular part of the speech (structure)?* At this part of the speech, he is developing

the problem before he offers a solution. As he develops the problem, he evokes sympathy.

- **Point 3/Evidence:**
  - *What is another important point FDR uses to develop his central idea?* **Point 3:** FDR explains a hopeful future via government involvement. **Evidence:** "But it is not in despair I paint you that picture . . . government is competent . . . ."
  - *How does this point develop the central idea?* It explains how the nation can address the concerns of all of its citizens, even those in poverty.
  - *What techniques are used to develop his point? How does this technique develop his point?* He revisits the personified comfort, opportunism, and timidity to remind the audience about the problem of prosperity within his solution for more government involvement. He uses positive word connotations when referring to the government and the American people ("men and women of good will," "warm hearts of dedication," "competent," "effective"). He refers to the government as effective and competent to build trust (ethos appeal).
  - *Why is this point where it is in the document (structure)? How does it help develop the central idea?* This point includes his closing where he offers a solution for the American people—come together with the government to address the problems of both comfortable prosperity and poverty.

- **Structure:**
  - *What is the overall structure of the document?* Problem-solution.

- **Implications:**
  - *What are the implications/consequences of this document?* This speech set the stage for many of FDR's initiatives. During his second term, Congress passed the Housing Act, laws were made to establish minimum wage (Fair Labor Standards Act), and more than 3.3 million jobs were developed through WPA (Works Progress Administration).

- **Evaluation:**
  - *How effective is the author in using sufficient, relevant evidence to develop a central idea?* Roosevelt is somewhat effective in supporting the central idea that America will continue on toward progress by addressing the concerns of all. He speaks of the problem of progress and prosperity in general terms, but allows the audience to consider the problem through the present context. He provides a sufficient amount of evi-

dence for stating the problems of poverty through the repetition of "I see" statements, and he effectively explains how the government and the American people can work together to address the concerns of all.

FRANKLIN D. ROOSEVELT'S SECOND INAUGURAL ADDRESS

Delivered January 20, 1937

. . . Among men of good will, science and democracy together offer an ever-richer life and ever-larger satisfaction to the individual. With this change in our moral climate and our rediscovered ability to improve our economic order, we have set our feet upon the road of enduring progress.

Shall we pause now and turn our back upon the road that lies ahead? Shall we call this the promised land? Or, shall we continue on our way? For "each age is a dream that is dying, or one that is coming to birth."

Many voices are heard as we face a great decision. Comfort says, "Tarry a while." Opportunism says, "This is a good spot." Timidity asks, "How difficult is the road ahead?"

True, we have come far from the days of stagnation and despair. Vitality has been preserved. Courage and confidence have been restored. Mental and moral horizons have been extended.

But our present gains were won under the pressure of more than ordinary circumstances. Advance became imperative under the goad of fear and suffering. The times were on the side of progress.

To hold to progress today, however, is more difficult. Dulled conscience, irresponsibility, and ruthless self-interest already reappear. Such symptoms of prosperity may become portents of disaster! Prosperity already tests the persistence of our progressive purpose.

Let us ask again: Have we reached the goal of our vision of that fourth day of March 1933? Have we found our happy valley?

I see a great nation, upon a great continent, blessed with a great wealth of natural resources. Its hundred and thirty million people are at peace among themselves; they are making their country a good neighbor among the nations. I see a United States which can demonstrate that, under democratic methods of government, national wealth can be translated into a spreading volume of human comforts hitherto unknown, and the lowest standard of living can be raised far above the level of mere subsistence.

But here is the challenge to our democracy: In this nation I see tens of millions of its citizens—a substantial part of its whole population—who at this very moment are denied the greater part of what the very lowest standards of today call the necessities of life.

I see millions of families trying to live on incomes so meager that the pall of family disaster hangs over them day by day.

I see millions whose daily lives in city and on farm continue under conditions labeled indecent by a so-called polite society half a century ago.

I see millions denied education, recreation, and the opportunity to better their lot and the lot of their children.

I see millions lacking the means to buy the products of farm and factory and by their poverty denying work and productiveness to many other millions.

I see one-third of a nation ill-housed, ill-clad, ill-nourished.

But it is not in despair that I paint you that picture. I paint it for you in hope—because the nation, seeing and understanding the injustice in it, proposes to paint it out. We are determined to make every American citizen the subject of his country's interest and concern; and we will never regard any faithful law-abiding group within our borders as superfluous. The test of our progress is not whether we add more to the abundance of those who have much; it is whether we provide enough for those who have too little.

If I know aught of the spirit and purpose of our Nation, we will not listen to comfort, opportunism, and timidity. We will carry on.

Overwhelmingly, we of the Republic are men and women of good will; men and women who have more than warm hearts of dedication; men and women who have cool heads and willing hands of practical purpose as well. They will insist that every agency of popular government use effective instruments to carry out their will.

Government is competent when all who compose it work as trustees for the whole people. It can make constant progress when it keeps abreast of all the facts. It can obtain justified support and legitimate criticism when the people receive true information of all that government does.

If I know aught of the will of our people, they will demand that these conditions of effective government shall be created and maintained. They will demand a nation uncorrupted by cancers of injustice and, therefore, strong among the nations in its example of the will to peace.

Today we reconsecrate our country to long-cherished ideals in a suddenly changed civilization. In every land there are always at work forces that drive men apart and forces that draw men together. In our personal ambitions we are individualists. But in our seeking for economic and political progress as a nation, we all go up, or else we all go down, as one people.

Appendix B

Blank Models and Guides

BLANK LITERARY ANALYSIS WHEEL

Directions: Draw arrows across elements to show connections.

Text: _____

Purpose/Context

Setting

Mood

Language
Structure
Style

Symbols

Plot/
Conflict

Characters

Theme

Point of View

Tone

Interpretation

Created by Tamra Stambaugh, Ph.D., & Emily Mofield, Ed.D., 2015.

LITERARY ANALYSIS WHEEL GUIDE

Text: _____

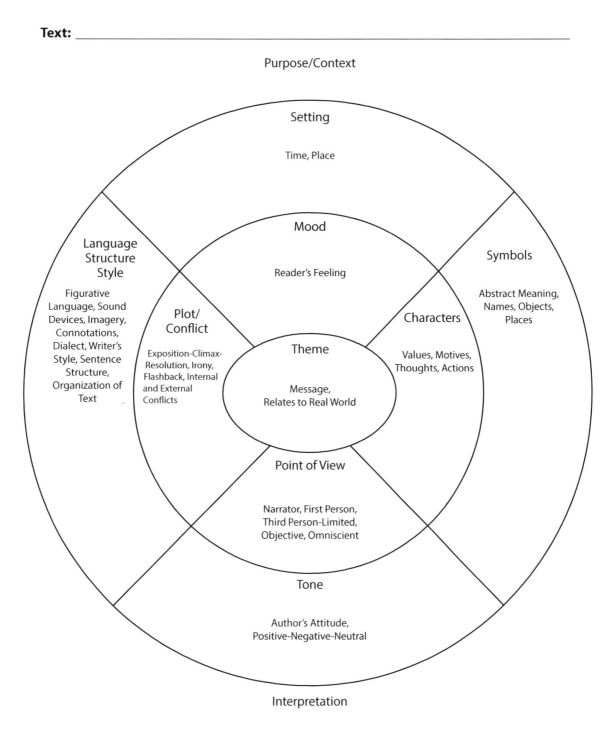

Purpose/Context

Setting

Time, Place

Mood

Reader's Feeling

Language
Structure
Style

Figurative
Language, Sound
Devices, Imagery,
Connotations,
Dialect, Writer's
Style, Sentence
Structure,
Organization of
Text

Symbols

Abstract Meaning,
Names, Objects,
Places

Plot/
Conflict

Exposition-Climax-
Resolution, Irony,
Flashback, Internal
and External
Conflicts

Theme

Message,
Relates to Real World

Characters

Values, Motives,
Thoughts, Actions

Point of View

Narrator, First Person,
Third Person-Limited,
Objective, Omniscient

Tone

Author's Attitude,
Positive-Negative-Neutral

Interpretation

Created by Tamra Stambaugh, Ph.D., & Emily Mofield, Ed.D., 2015.

BLANK VISUAL ANALYSIS WHEEL

Directions: Draw arrows across elements to show connections.

Art Piece: _____

Purpose/Context

Point of View

Images

Techniques

Emotions

Main Idea

Artist Background

Structure/ Organization

Implications

Evaluation

Created by Tamra Stambaugh, Ph.D., & Emily Mofield, Ed.D., 2015.

VISUAL ANALYSIS WHEEL GUIDE

Art Piece: _____

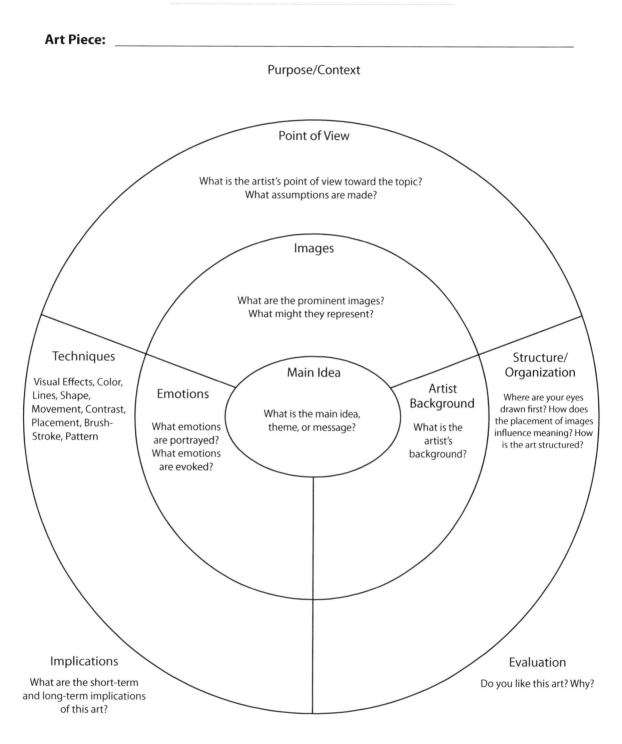

Purpose/Context

Point of View

What is the artist's point of view toward the topic?
What assumptions are made?

Images

What are the prominent images?
What might they represent?

Techniques

Visual Effects, Color, Lines, Shape, Movement, Contrast, Placement, Brush-Stroke, Pattern

Main Idea

What is the main idea, theme, or message?

Emotions

What emotions are portrayed? What emotions are evoked?

Artist Background

What is the artist's background?

Structure/ Organization

Where are your eyes drawn first? How does the placement of images influence meaning? How is the art structured?

Implications

What are the short-term and long-term implications of this art?

Evaluation

Do you like this art? Why?

Created by Tamra Stambaugh, Ph.D., & Emily Mofield, Ed.D., 2015.

BLANK RHETORICAL ANALYSIS WHEEL

Directions: Draw arrows across elements to show connections.

Text: _____

Purpose/Context

Point of View

Logos

Techniques

Claim

Pathos

Ethos

Structure/
Organization

Implications

Evaluation

Created by Emily Mofield, Ed.D., & Tamra Stambaugh, Ph.D., 2015.

RHETORICAL ANALYSIS WHEEL GUIDE

Text: _____

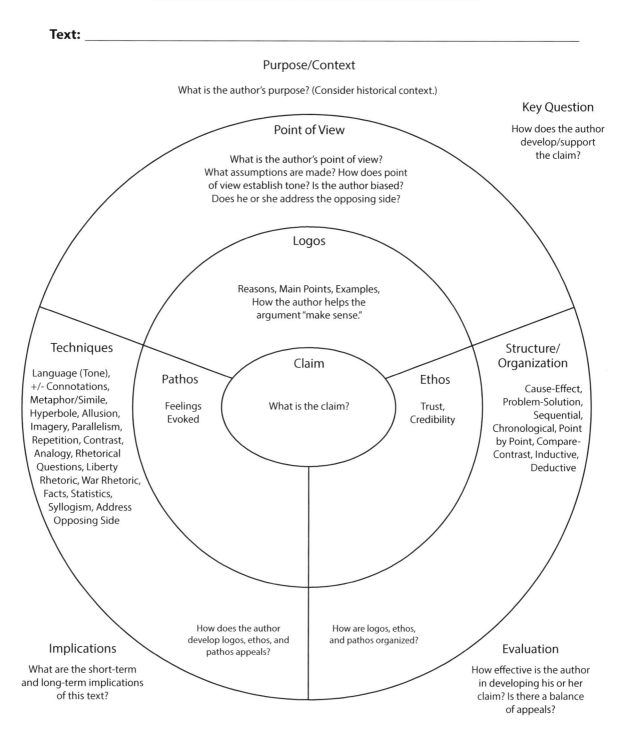

Purpose/Context

What is the author's purpose? (Consider historical context.)

Key Question

How does the author develop/support the claim?

Point of View

What is the author's point of view? What assumptions are made? How does point of view establish tone? Is the author biased? Does he or she address the opposing side?

Logos

Reasons, Main Points, Examples, How the author helps the argument "make sense."

Techniques

Language (Tone), +/- Connotations, Metaphor/Simile, Hyperbole, Allusion, Imagery, Parallelism, Repetition, Contrast, Analogy, Rhetorical Questions, Liberty Rhetoric, War Rhetoric, Facts, Statistics, Syllogism, Address Opposing Side

Pathos

Feelings Evoked

Claim

What is the claim?

Ethos

Trust, Credibility

Structure/ Organization

Cause-Effect, Problem-Solution, Sequential, Chronological, Point by Point, Compare-Contrast, Inductive, Deductive

Implications

What are the short-term and long-term implications of this text?

How does the author develop logos, ethos, and pathos appeals?

How are logos, ethos, and pathos organized?

Evaluation

How effective is the author in developing his or her claim? Is there a balance of appeals?

Created by Emily Mofield, Ed.D., & Tamra Stambaugh, Ph.D., 2015.

BLANK TEXT ANALYSIS WHEEL

Directions: Draw arrows across elements to show connections.

Text: _____

Purpose/Context

Point of View

Point #1

Evidence

Techniques

Central Idea

Point #2

Point #3

Structure/
Organization

Evidence

Evidence

Implications

Evaluation

Created by Emily Mofield, Ed.D., & Tamra Stambaugh, Ph.D., 2015.

TEXT ANALYSIS WHEEL GUIDE

Text: _____

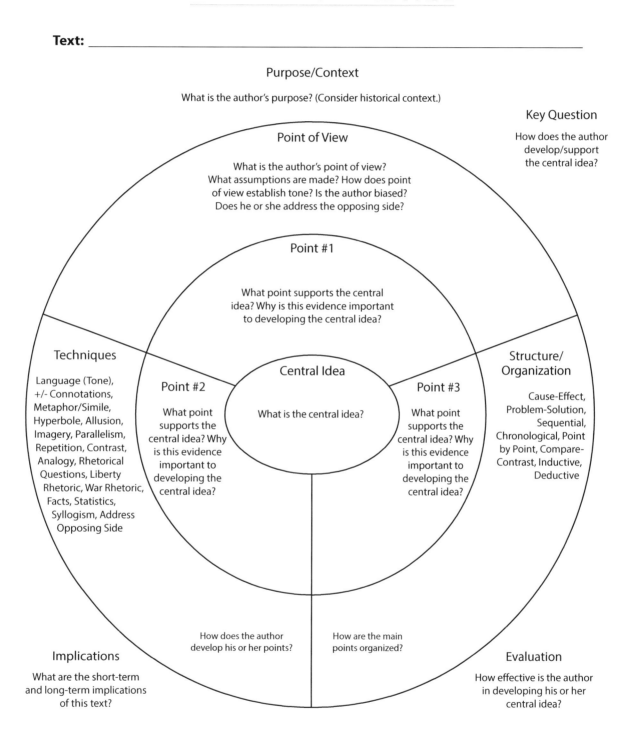

Purpose/Context

What is the author's purpose? (Consider historical context.)

Key Question

How does the author develop/support the central idea?

Point of View

What is the author's point of view? What assumptions are made? How does point of view establish tone? Is the author biased? Does he or she address the opposing side?

Point #1

What point supports the central idea? Why is this evidence important to developing the central idea?

Techniques

Language (Tone), +/- Connotations, Metaphor/Simile, Hyperbole, Allusion, Imagery, Parallelism, Repetition, Contrast, Analogy, Rhetorical Questions, Liberty Rhetoric, War Rhetoric, Facts, Statistics, Syllogism, Address Opposing Side

Point #2

What point supports the central idea? Why is this evidence important to developing the central idea?

Central Idea

What is the central idea?

Point #3

What point supports the central idea? Why is this evidence important to developing the central idea?

Structure/Organization

Cause-Effect, Problem-Solution, Sequential, Chronological, Point by Point, Compare-Contrast, Inductive, Deductive

Implications

What are the short-term and long-term implications of this text?

How does the author develop his or her points?

How are the main points organized?

Evaluation

How effective is the author in developing his or her central idea?

Created by Emily Mofield, Ed.D., & Tamra Stambaugh, Ph.D., 2015.

BIG IDEA REFLECTION

What?	**Concepts:** What concepts/ideas are in the text?	
	Generalizations: What broad statement can you make about one or more of these concepts? Make it generalizable beyond the text.	
	Issue: What is the main issue, problem, or conflict?	
So What?	**Insight:** What insight on life is provided from this text?	
	World/Community/Individual: How does this text relate to you, your community, or your world? What question does the author want you to ask yourself?	
Now What?	**Implications:** How should you respond to the ideas in the text? What action should you take? What are the implications of the text? What can you do with this information?	

Created by Emily Mofield, Ed.D., & Tamra Stambaugh, Ph.D., 2015.

REASONING ABOUT A SITUATION OR EVENT

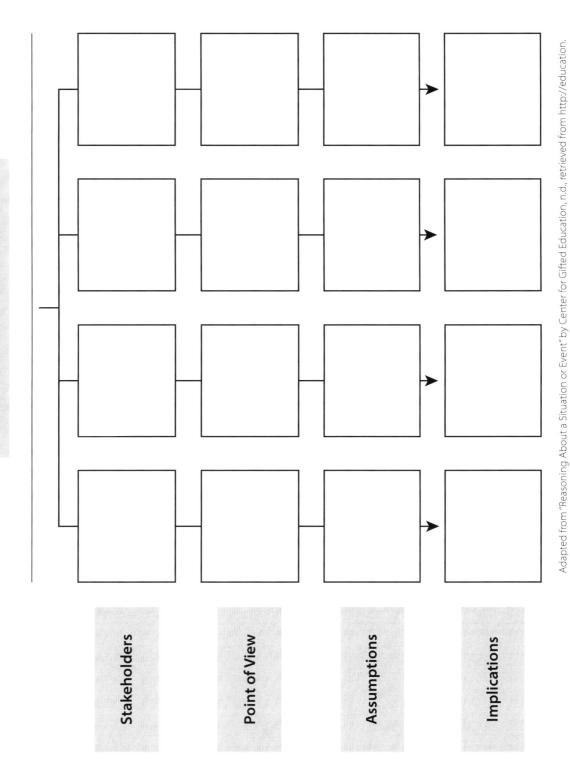

What Is the Situation?

Stakeholders

Point of View

Assumptions

Implications

CONCEPT ORGANIZER

Directions: How does each work exemplify each generalization? What new generalization can you make?

Literature, Art, or Media:	Literature, Art, or Media:	Literature, Art, or Media:
Perception of truth* varies. (*"Truth" and "reality" can be interchanged to fit the context of the work.)		
There are negatives and positives in realizing truth.		
There are consequences to believing perception rather than truth.		
Examine the relationship between truth, perception, power, ignorance, happiness, perspective, and/or freedom.		

Appendix C
Rubrics

RUBRIC 1: PRODUCT RUBRIC

Name: _____   Date: _____   Lesson: _____

	Unacceptable/ Needs Improvement	Fair	Acceptable	Excellent
Completion	Not turned in or late.	Missing key pieces.	Completed but lacks thought and professionalism.	Satisfactorily meets all requirements and expectations of the task.
Concept/ Content	Limited or vague connection.	Little connection from lesson content is made to the theme of truth.	Accurately relates lesson content and concept of truth to assignment.	Insightfully relates lesson content and concept of truth to assignment.
Thinking	Limited or vague evidence	Reasoning is inaccurate/ Lacks originality, logical conclusions, or substantial claims.	Demonstrates some evidence of higher level thinking (creativity, evaluation, or analysis).	Demonstrates substantial evidence of higher level thinking (creativity, analysis, or evaluation with evidence).
Student-Developed Criteria				

Comments:

217

RUBRIC 2: COMPARISON ESSAY RUBRIC

Name: _____   Date: _____   Lesson: _____

	Unacceptable/ Needs Improvement	Fair	Acceptable	Exemplary
Includes an appropriate introduction and thesis statement.				
Provides at least three examples from Text 1 to support comparison.				
Provides at least three examples from Text 2 to support comparison.				
Uses at least three direct quotes to support arguments.				
Thoughtfully includes commentary to explain significance of the examples.				
Conclusion revisits thesis statement and provides a logical deduction about the works.				
Uses appropriate grammar and mechanics throughout.				

Comments:

RUBRIC 3: COLLAGE RUBRIC

Name: _____ Date: _____ Lesson: _____

	Unacceptable/ Needs Improvement	Fair	Acceptable	Exemplary
All words and images are relevant to the theme and/or related text.				
The collage/media includes at least four quotes from newspapers, magazines, or computer-generated text supporting the theme in the text.				
Collage/media includes at least four quotes from text studied.				
The collage/media includes at least eight symbolic elements representing theme.				
The images and words are arranged thoughtfully to enhance the design and layout of the collage/media.				
A written description is included explaining each symbolic element and how the pictures and quotes support a selected theme.				
The collage/media includes adequate detail about the selected theme.				
The content of the collage/media is interesting and visually appealing.				
The collage/media communicates the student's understanding of theme.				
The collage includes a creative title to support the theme and text.				
Total				

Comments:

RUBRIC 4: SOUNDTRACK RUBRIC

Name: _____ Date: _____ Lesson: _____

Category	Unacceptable/ Needs Improvement	Fair	Acceptable	Exemplary
Relevance	CD or playlist includes 1–2 relevant songs to the plot elements and/or theme in the text.	CD or playlist includes only 3–4 relevant songs to the plot elements and/or theme in the text.	CD or playlist includes at least 5–7 relevant songs to the plot elements and/or theme in the text.	CD or playlist includes at least eight relevant songs to the plot elements and/or theme in the text.
Music Explanation	Does not explain the lyrics or mood of selected songs.	Includes titles and artists for some songs. Provides a fair explanation of the lyric's meaning. Includes cited lyrics for only 3–4 songs. Explanations lack depth and detail. If there are no lyrics in the song, includes only a lacking description of the mood of the song and how this mood is created by the music	Includes titles and artists an adequate explanation of the lyrics' meaning in adequate detail. Includes cited lyrics. If there are no lyrics in the song, includes an adequate description of the mood of the song and how this mood is created by the music.	Includes titles and artists for all songs selected. Includes cited lyrics for each of the eight songs with a thoughtful, insightful explanation of the lyrics' meaning. If there are no lyrics in the song, includes a detailed, in-depth description of the mood of the song and how this mood is created by the music.

Rubric 4, Continued

Category	Unacceptable/ Needs Improvement	Fair	Acceptable	Exemplary
Connection to Text Explanation	Includes an explanation of how the songs are related to the text with only 1–2 direct quotes from the text followed by an explanation.	Includes an explanation of how the songs are related to the text with only 3–4 direct quotes from the text followed by an explanation.	Includes an explanation of how the songs are related to the text with five direct quotes from the text followed by an explanation.	Includes an explanation of how the songs are related to the text using at least eight direct text quotes (one quote for each song) followed by an explanation.
Title	No title provided.	Title is trite or clichéd and reveals little insight into the ideas in the album.	Title is thoughtful, revealing some insight into the ideas presented in the album.	Includes a creative, original title that reveals insight into the ideas presented in the soundtrack album.
Cover	No cover is provided.	More detail is needed to convey the ideas presented in the album. Cover is not attractive or well-designed.	Includes a somewhat attractive cover that conveys the ideas presented in the album with acceptable personal artwork or computer graphics. Cover could be a little more polished. Mostly matches the theme and tone of the album.	Includes a well-designed, attractive, artistic album cover made from appealing computer graphics or attractive detailed personal artwork. Cover matches the theme and tone of the album.

Comments:

RUBRIC 5: CULMINATING PROJECT RUBRIC

Name: _____   Date: _____

	Unacceptable/ Needs Improvement	Fair	Acceptable	Exemplary
Completion	Not turned in or late.	Missing key pieces.	Completed but lacks thought and professionalism.	Satisfactorily meets all requirements and expectations of the task.
Evidence	Limited or no evidence.	Little support or elaboration to support ideas and generalizations.	Gives support/ elaboration to support ideas.	Gives meaningful support/ elaboration to support ideas and generalizations.
Concept	Limited or vague connection.	Little connection from unit content is made to the theme of truth versus perception.	Accurately relates ideas of truth versus perception to assignment.	Insightfully relates the theme of truth versus perception to assignment.
Content	Limited or no content application.	Vague connections are made to content.	Some connections are made to content with some evidence.	Synthesizes content across lessons with substantial support and evidence.
Process	Limited or vague evidence	Reasoning is inaccurate/lacks originality, logical conclusions, or substantial claims.	Demonstrates some evidence of higher level thinking (creativity, evaluation, or analysis).	Provides insightful evidence to support higher level thinking (creativity, evaluation, or analysis) in developing complex conclusions.
Student-Developed Criteria				

Comments:

Appendix D

Teacher's Novel Guides

TEACHER'S GUIDE TO HANDOUT 6.2

Symbol	Meaning	Other Literary Significance	Later Reference(s)
Adam and Eve, tree of knowledge, apple (March 12)	Apple = knowledge. Eating from the tree of knowledge was a result of *deception* from the serpent. Eating the tree opened their eyes to their nakedness—disillusionment.	Allusion: Reference to Garden of Eden in Genesis.	*Paradise Lost* (Oct. 5).
Robinson Crusoe (March 30)	Isolation; smart with no friends.	Foreshadowing: Charlie later feels emotionally alone. Allusion: Reference to book.	End of May 20: "Now I'm more alone than ever before."
Wax fruit (second April entry)	Relates to Adam and Eve: fake fruit, fake knowledge, Charlie has fake intelligence.	Allusion: Reference to Garden of Eden.	
Sta-brite metal polish (April 21)	Stay bright—will his intelligence stay bright?	Foreshadows that this is a fundamental question in the novel. Irony: This not a good-luck piece.	
Three blind mice, carving knife (May 3)	Blind, alludes to ways of being blind—the bewilderments of the eyes are of two kinds—going into the light and out of the light. Charlie has been blinded by being "ignorant" and by painfully experiencing life as a smart man. Carving knife = surgeon's knife.	Characterization: Shows Charlie's experience of disillusionment	May 20: "There's no going back . . . I'm like a man born blind"; June 20: Carving knife = desire for mom to hurt Charlie.
Picasso's *Mother and Child* (May 25)	Alice acting as a mothering figure (part of her internal conflict).	Characterization of Alice.	

Symbol	Meaning	Other Literary Significance	Later Reference(s)
Courtier, masked, sword, protecting	Could Charlie be her protecting hero? Mask—who is the real Charlie?	Characterization of Alice and Charlie.	May 25: The maiden held the sword. Alice was the authority figure over Charlie, which reflects Charlie's fear of intimacy.
Norma	Normal child.	Characterization of Norma.	
Rose	Seemingly good mother—wanting to have her family appear normal, which relates to appearance theme. Roses have thorns, as Rose has evil characteristics.	Characterization of Rose.	
IQ of 185 and 70, distance (End of June 6)	IQ does not equal emotional intelligence.	Irony: No matter what his level of intelligence, he is not close to Alice.	
Window (June 10)	Barrier between old and new Charlie.	Characterization: Internal conflict.	Right before June 20: Faye "lived out the window"—barrier.
Behavior of Algernon throughout the novel	Charlie's progress and behavior.	Foreshadowing: What happens to Algernon happens to Charlie.	June 21: Success is reward for Charlie; food is a reward for Algernon.
"Algernon was glaring . . . reflection in the mirror." (June 13)	Algernon symbolizes Charlie. The mirror symbolizes Charlie examining his own self, past, present, and thinking about his future.	Characterization of Charlie.	June 20: Matt studied Charlie in the mirror—insight into this past. "In the mirror I watched the bright red bubble and the thin line . . ." is symbolic of looking into his painful past. More mirror imagery in June 20: looking at infinite self—who is the real Charlie?

TEACHER'S GUIDE TO HANDOUT 9.2

Symbol	Meaning	Other Literary Significance	Later Reference(s)
Pigeon-winged books	Freedom: Books/knowledge bring freedom to the mind (as birds are free to fly).	Foreshadows that this will free Montag.	
Hearth and the Salamander	Dual function of fire: Fire can be warming and comforting as Montag feels comfortable in his job. A salamander in mythology can withstand fire. Foreshadows Montag going through adversity and surviving.	Foreshadows Montag's adversity. Allusion to mythology.	
Sieve and the Sand	He cannot comprehend the knowledge adequately or understand its great importance, though he wants to (just as sand cannot be contained in a sieve).	Characterization of Montag	
White imagery	Clarisse is associated with white (milk, light, etc.), representing purity, alluding to the freed prisoner in Plato's Allegory.	Foreshadows that Montag will be brought out into the light. Allusion: Freed prisoner in Plato's allegory.	Several descriptions of Clarisse throughout contrast with Mildred's descriptions.
Machine imagery (Mechanical Hound)	People act robotically in society because they are not really thinking for themselves.		
Carnival imagery (masks)	People in this society are not really happy, they only think they are happy (like the prisoners in Plato's cave). The masks represent a false identity, an illusion of what is real.		
Mirror	The book itself is a mirror for the reader—the reader must consider how the book mirrors society.		
Phoenix	Rebirth of society, rebirth of Montag as a person.	Allusion to mythology: Phoenix bird burns and is reborn.	Relates to the allusions of Ecclesiastes ("a time to be born . . .").

About the Authors

Emily Mofield, Ed.D., is the lead consulting teacher for gifted education for Sumner County Schools in Tennessee and is involved in supporting several projects with Vanderbilt Programs for Talented Youth. She has also taught as a gifted education language arts middle school teacher for 10 years. Her work is devoted to developing challenging differentiated curriculum for gifted learners and addressing their social/emotional needs. Emily regularly presents professional development on effective differentiation for advanced learners. She is a national board certified teacher in Language Arts and has been recognized as the Tennessee Association for Gifted Children Teacher of the Year.

Tamra Stambaugh, Ph.D., is an assistant research professor in special education and executive director of Programs for Talented Youth at Vanderbilt University Peabody College. She received her Ph.D. in Educational Policy, Planning, and Leadership with an emphasis in gifted education from William & Mary. She is the coauthor/editor of several books including *Serving Gifted Students in Rural Settings* (coedited with Susannah Wood), *Comprehensive Curriculum for Gifted Learners* (with Joyce VanTassel-Baska), *Overlooked Gems: A National Perspective on Low-Income Promising Students* (with Joyce VanTassel-Baska), *Leading Change in Gifted Education* (with Bronwyn MacFarlane), the *Jacob's Ladder Reading Comprehension Program Series* (with Joyce VanTassel-Baska and Kim Chandler), and *Practical Solutions for Underrepresented Gifted Students: Effective Curriculum* (with Kim Chandler), as well as numerous book chapters and research articles. Stambaugh's research interests focus on talent development support structures for gifted students and key curriculum and instructional interventions that support gifted learners—especially those students from rural backgrounds and those from poverty.

Common Core State Standards Alignment

Lesson	Common Core State Standards in ELA/Literacy
Lesson 1	SL.8.2 Analyze the purpose of information presented in diverse media and formats (e.g., visually, quantitatively, orally) and evaluate the motives (e.g., social, commercial, political) behind its presentation.
	SL.9-10.1 Initiate and participate effectively in a range of collaborative discussions (one-on-one, in groups, and teacher-led) with diverse partners on grades 9–10 topics, texts, and issues, building on others' ideas and expressing their own clearly and persuasively.
	SL.9-10.1c Propel conversations by posing and responding to questions that relate the current discussion to broader themes or larger ideas; actively incorporate others into the discussion; and clarify, verify, or challenge ideas and conclusions.
	SL.9-10.1d Respond thoughtfully to diverse perspectives, summarize points of agreement and disagreement, and, when warranted, qualify or justify their own views and understanding and make new connections in light of the evidence and reasoning presented.
	W.9-10.4 Produce clear and coherent writing in which the development, organization, and style are appropriate to task, purpose, and audience
	RI.9-10.7 Analyze various accounts of a subject told in different mediums (e.g., a person's life story in both print and multimedia), determining which details are emphasized in each account.
	W.9-10.4 Produce clear and coherent writing in which the development, organization, and style are appropriate to task, purpose, and audience.
	W.9-10.5 Develop and strengthen writing as needed by planning, revising, editing, rewriting, or trying a new approach, focusing on addressing what is most significant for a specific purpose and audience.

Lesson	Common Core State Standards in ELA/Literacy
Lesson 2	RL.9-10.1 Cite strong and thorough textual evidence to support analysis of what the text says explicitly as well as inferences drawn from the text.
	RL.9-10.2 Determine a theme or central idea of a text and analyze in detail its development over the course of the text, including how it emerges and is shaped and refined by specific details; provide an objective summary of the text.
	RL.9-10.6 Analyze a particular point of view or cultural experience reflected in a work of literature from outside the United States, drawing on a wide reading of world literature.
	RI.9-10.2 Determine a central idea of a text and analyze its development over the course of the text, including how it emerges and is shaped and refined by specific details; provide an objective summary of the text.
	SL.9-10.1 Initiate and participate effectively in a range of collaborative discussions (one-on-one, in groups, and teacher-led) with diverse partners on grades 9–10 topics, texts, and issues, building on others' ideas and expressing their own clearly and persuasively.
	SL.9-10.1c Propel conversations by posing and responding to questions that relate the current discussion to broader themes or larger ideas; actively incorporate others into the discussion; and clarify, verify, or challenge ideas and conclusions.
	SL.9-10.1d Respond thoughtfully to diverse perspectives, summarize points of agreement and disagreement, and, when warranted, qualify or justify their own views and understanding and make new connections in light of the evidence and reasoning presented.
	W.9-10.4 Produce clear and coherent writing in which the development, organization, and style are appropriate to task, purpose, and audience.
	W.9-10.5 Develop and strengthen writing as needed by planning, revising, editing, rewriting, or trying a new approach, focusing on addressing what is most significant for a specific purpose and audience.
Lesson 3	RL.9-10.1 Cite strong and thorough textual evidence to support analysis of what the text says explicitly as well as inferences drawn from the text.
	RL.9-10.2 Determine a theme or central idea of a text and analyze in detail its development over the course of the text, including how it emerges and is shaped and refined by specific details; provide an objective summary of the text.
	RL.9-10.3 Analyze how complex characters (e.g., those with multiple or conflicting motivations) develop over the course of a text, interact with other characters, and advance the plot or develop the theme.
	RL.9-10.4 Determine the meaning of words and phrases as they are used in the text, including figurative and connotative meanings; analyze the cumulative impact of specific word choices on meaning and tone (e.g., how the language evokes a sense of time and place; how it sets a formal or informal tone).
	RL.9-10.5 Analyze how an author's choices concerning how to structure a text, order events within it (e.g., parallel plots), and manipulate time (e.g., pacing, flashbacks) create such effects as mystery, tension, or surprise.

Lesson	Common Core State Standards in ELA/Literacy
Lesson 3, *continued*	SL.9-10.1 Initiate and participate effectively in a range of collaborative discussions (one-on-one, in groups, and teacher-led) with diverse partners on grades 9–10 topics, texts, and issues, building on others' ideas and expressing their own clearly and persuasively.
	SL.9-10.1c Propel conversations by posing and responding to questions that relate the current discussion to broader themes or larger ideas; actively incorporate others into the discussion; and clarify, verify, or challenge ideas and conclusions.
	SL.9-10.1d Respond thoughtfully to diverse perspectives, summarize points of agreement and disagreement, and, when warranted, qualify or justify their own views and understanding and make new connections in light of the evidence and reasoning presented.
	W.9-10.4 Produce clear and coherent writing in which the development, organization, and style are appropriate to task, purpose, and audience.
	W.9-10.5 Develop and strengthen writing as needed by planning, revising, editing, rewriting, or trying a new approach, focusing on addressing what is most significant for a specific purpose and audience.
Lesson 4	RI.9-10.7 Analyze various accounts of a subject told in different mediums (e.g., a person's life story in both print and multimedia), determining which details are emphasized in each account.
	RH.9-10.1 Cite specific textual evidence to support analysis of primary and secondary sources, attending to such features as the date and origin of the information.
	SL.8.2 Analyze the purpose of information presented in diverse media and formats (e.g., visually, quantitatively, orally) and evaluate the motives (e.g., social, commercial, political) behind its presentation.
	SL.9-10.1 Initiate and participate effectively in a range of collaborative discussions (one-on-one, in groups, and teacher-led) with diverse partners on grades 9–10 topics, texts, and issues, building on others' ideas and expressing their own clearly and persuasively.
	SL.9-10.1c Propel conversations by posing and responding to questions that relate the current discussion to broader themes or larger ideas; actively incorporate others into the discussion; and clarify, verify, or challenge ideas and conclusions.
	SL.9-10.1d Respond thoughtfully to diverse perspectives, summarize points of agreement and disagreement, and, when warranted, qualify or justify their own views and understanding and make new connections in light of the evidence and reasoning presented.
	W.9-10.4 Produce clear and coherent writing in which the development, organization, and style are appropriate to task, purpose, and audience
	W.9-10.5 Develop and strengthen writing as needed by planning, revising, editing, rewriting, or trying a new approach, focusing on addressing what is most significant for a specific purpose and audience.

Lesson	Common Core State Standards in ELA/Literacy
Lesson 5	RI.9-10.1 Cite strong and thorough textual evidence to support analysis of what the text says explicitly as well as inferences drawn from the text.
	RI.9-10.2 Determine a central idea of a text and analyze its development over the course of the text, including how it emerges and is shaped and refined by specific details; provide an objective summary of the text.
	RI.9-10.3 Analyze how the author unfolds an analysis or series of ideas or events, including the order in which the points are made, how they are introduced and developed, and the connections that are drawn between them.
	RI.9-10.4 Determine the meaning of words and phrases as they are used in a text, including figurative, connotative, and technical meanings; analyze the cumulative impact of specific word choices on meaning and tone (e.g., how the language of a court opinion differs from that of a newspaper).
	RI.9-10.5 Analyze in detail how an author's ideas or claims are developed and refined by particular sentences, paragraphs, or larger portions of a text (e.g., a section or chapter).
	RI.9-10.6 Determine an author's point of view or purpose in a text and analyze how an author uses rhetoric to advance that point of view or purpose.
	RI.9-10.9 Analyze seminal U.S. documents of historical and literary significance (e.g., Washington's Farewell Address, the Gettysburg Address, Roosevelt's Four Freedoms speech, King's Letter from Birmingham Jail), including how they address related themes and concepts.
	RH.9-10.1 Cite specific textual evidence to support analysis of primary and secondary sources, attending to such features as the date and origin of the information.
	SL.9-10.1 Initiate and participate effectively in a range of collaborative discussions (one-on-one, in groups, and teacher-led) with diverse partners on grades 9–10 topics, texts, and issues, building on others' ideas and expressing their own clearly and persuasively.
	RH.9-10.2 Determine the central ideas or information of a primary or secondary source; provide an accurate summary of how key events or ideas develop over the course of the text.RH.9-10.5 Analyze how a text uses structure to emphasize key points or advance an explanation or analysis.
	RH.9-10.6 Compare the point of view of two or more authors for how they treat the same or similar topics, including which details they include and emphasize in their respective accounts.
	RH.9-10.8 Assess the extent to which the reasoning and evidence in a text support the author's claims.
	RH.9-10.9 Compare and contrast treatments of the same topic in several primary and secondary sources.
	SL.9-10.1c Propel conversations by posing and responding to questions that relate the current discussion to broader themes or larger ideas; actively incorporate others into the discussion; and clarify, verify, or challenge ideas and conclusions.
	SL.9-10.1d Respond thoughtfully to diverse perspectives, summarize points of agreement and disagreement, and, when warranted, qualify or justify their own views and understanding and make new connections in light of the evidence and reasoning presented.

Lesson	Common Core State Standards in ELA/Literacy
Lesson 5, *continued*	SL.9-10.4 Present information, findings, and supporting evidence clearly, concisely, and logically such that listeners can follow the line of reasoning and the organization, development, substance, and style are appropriate to purpose, audience, and task.
	W.9-10.4 Produce clear and coherent writing in which the development, organization, and style are appropriate to task, purpose, and audience.
	W.9-10.5 Develop and strengthen writing as needed by planning, revising, editing, rewriting, or trying a new approach, focusing on addressing what is most significant for a specific purpose and audience.
Lesson 6	RL.9-10.1 Cite strong and thorough textual evidence to support analysis of what the text says explicitly as well as inferences drawn from the text.
	RL.9-10.2 Determine a theme or central idea of a text and analyze in detail its development over the course of the text, including how it emerges and is shaped and refined by specific details; provide an objective summary of the text.
	RL.9-10.3 Analyze how complex characters (e.g., those with multiple or conflicting motivations) develop over the course of a text, interact with other characters, and advance the plot or develop the theme.
	RL.9-10.4 Determine the meaning of words and phrases as they are used in the text, including figurative and connotative meanings; analyze the cumulative impact of specific word choices on meaning and tone (e.g., how the language evokes a sense of time and place; how it sets a formal or informal tone).
	RL.9-10.5 Analyze how an author's choices concerning how to structure a text, order events within it (e.g., parallel plots), and manipulate time (e.g., pacing, flashbacks) create such effects as mystery, tension, or surprise.
	SL.9-10.1 Initiate and participate effectively in a range of collaborative discussions (one-on-one, in groups, and teacher-led) with diverse partners on grades 9–10 topics, texts, and issues, building on others' ideas and expressing their own clearly and persuasively.
	SL.9-10.1c Propel conversations by posing and responding to questions that relate the current discussion to broader themes or larger ideas; actively incorporate others into the discussion; and clarify, verify, or challenge ideas and conclusions.
	SL.9-10.1d Respond thoughtfully to diverse perspectives, summarize points of agreement and disagreement, and, when warranted, qualify or justify their own views and understanding and make new connections in light of the evidence and reasoning presented.
	W.9-10.4 Produce clear and coherent writing in which the development, organization, and style are appropriate to task, purpose, and audience.
	W.9-10.5 Develop and strengthen writing as needed by planning, revising, editing, rewriting, or trying a new approach, focusing on addressing what is most significant for a specific purpose and audience.
Lesson 7	RL.9-10.1 Cite strong and thorough textual evidence to support analysis of what the text says explicitly as well as inferences drawn from the text.
	RL.9-10.2 Determine a theme or central idea of a text and analyze in detail its development over the course of the text, including how it emerges and is shaped and refined by specific details; provide an objective summary of the text.

Lesson	Common Core State Standards in ELA/Literacy
Lesson 7, *continued*	RL.9-10.3 Analyze how complex characters (e.g., those with multiple or conflicting motivations) develop over the course of a text, interact with other characters, and advance the plot or develop the theme.
	RL.9-10.4 Determine the meaning of words and phrases as they are used in the text, including figurative and connotative meanings; analyze the cumulative impact of specific word choices on meaning and tone (e.g., how the language evokes a sense of time and place; how it sets a formal or informal tone).
	RL.9-10.5 Analyze how an author's choices concerning how to structure a text, order events within it (e.g., parallel plots), and manipulate time (e.g., pacing, flashbacks) create such effects as mystery, tension, or surprise.
	SL.9-10.1 Initiate and participate effectively in a range of collaborative discussions (one-on-one, in groups, and teacher-led) with diverse partners on grades 9–10 topics, texts, and issues, building on others' ideas and expressing their own clearly and persuasively.
	SL.9-10.1c Propel conversations by posing and responding to questions that relate the current discussion to broader themes or larger ideas; actively incorporate others into the discussion; and clarify, verify, or challenge ideas and conclusions.
	SL.9-10.1d Respond thoughtfully to diverse perspectives, summarize points of agreement and disagreement, and, when warranted, qualify or justify their own views and understanding and make new connections in light of the evidence and reasoning presented.
	W.9-10.4 Produce clear and coherent writing in which the development, organization, and style are appropriate to task, purpose, and audience.
	W.9-10.5 Develop and strengthen writing as needed by planning, revising, editing, rewriting, or trying a new approach, focusing on addressing what is most significant for a specific purpose and audience.
Lesson 8	RI.9-10.1 Cite strong and thorough textual evidence to support analysis of what the text says explicitly as well as inferences drawn from the text.
	RI.9-10.2 Determine a central idea of a text and analyze its development over the course of the text, including how it emerges and is shaped and refined by specific details; provide an objective summary of the text.
	RI.9-10.3 Analyze how the author unfolds an analysis or series of ideas or events, including the order in which the points are made, how they are introduced and developed, and the connections that are drawn between them.
	RI.9-10.4 Determine the meaning of words and phrases as they are used in a text, including figurative, connotative, and technical meanings; analyze the cumulative impact of specific word choices on meaning and tone (e.g., how the language of a court opinion differs from that of a newspaper).
	RI.9-10.5 Analyze in detail how an author's ideas or claims are developed and refined by particular sentences, paragraphs, or larger portions of a text (e.g., a section or chapter).
	RI.9-10.6 Determine an author's point of view or purpose in a text and analyze how an author uses rhetoric to advance that point of view or purpose.
	RH.9-10.1 Cite specific textual evidence to support analysis of primary and secondary sources, attending to such features as the date and origin of the information.

Lesson	Common Core State Standards in ELA/Literacy
Lesson 8, *continued*	RH.9-10.2 Determine the central ideas or information of a primary or secondary source; provide an accurate summary of how key events or ideas develop over the course of the text.
	RH.9-10.5 Analyze how a text uses structure to emphasize key points or advance an explanation or analysis.
	RH.9-10.6 Compare the point of view of two or more authors for how they treat the same or similar topics, including which details they include and emphasize in their respective accounts.
	RH.9-10.8 Assess the extent to which the reasoning and evidence in a text support the author's claims.
	RH.9-10.9 Compare and contrast treatments of the same topic in several primary and secondary sources.
	SL.8.2 Analyze the purpose of information presented in diverse media and formats (e.g., visually, quantitatively, orally) and evaluate the motives (e.g., social, commercial, political) behind its presentation.
	SL.9-10.1 Initiate and participate effectively in a range of collaborative discussions (one-on-one, in groups, and teacher-led) with diverse partners on grades 9–10 topics, texts, and issues, building on others' ideas and expressing their own clearly and persuasively.
	SL.9-10.1c Propel conversations by posing and responding to questions that relate the current discussion to broader themes or larger ideas; actively incorporate others into the discussion; and clarify, verify, or challenge ideas and conclusions.
	SL.9-10.1d Respond thoughtfully to diverse perspectives, summarize points of agreement and disagreement, and, when warranted, qualify or justify their own views and understanding and make new connections in light of the evidence and reasoning presented.
	SL.9-10.4 Present information, findings, and supporting evidence clearly, concisely, and logically such that listeners can follow the line of reasoning and the organization, development, substance, and style are appropriate to purpose, audience, and task.
	W.9-10.4 Produce clear and coherent writing in which the development, organization, and style are appropriate to task, purpose, and audience.
	W.9-10.5 Develop and strengthen writing as needed by planning, revising, editing, rewriting, or trying a new approach, focusing on addressing what is most significant for a specific purpose and audience.
Lesson 9	RL.9-10.1 Cite strong and thorough textual evidence to support analysis of what the text says explicitly as well as inferences drawn from the text.
	RL.9-10.2 Determine a theme or central idea of a text and analyze in detail its development over the course of the text, including how it emerges and is shaped and refined by specific details; provide an objective summary of the text.
	RL.9-10.3 Analyze how complex characters (e.g., those with multiple or conflicting motivations) develop over the course of a text, interact with other characters, and advance the plot or develop the theme.

Lesson	Common Core State Standards in ELA/Literacy
Lesson 9, *continued*	RL.9-10.4 Determine the meaning of words and phrases as they are used in the text, including figurative and connotative meanings; analyze the cumulative impact of specific word choices on meaning and tone (e.g., how the language evokes a sense of time and place; how it sets a formal or informal tone).
	RL.9-10.5 Analyze how an author's choices concerning how to structure a text, order events within it (e.g., parallel plots), and manipulate time (e.g., pacing, flashbacks) create such effects as mystery, tension, or surprise.
	SL.9-10.1 Initiate and participate effectively in a range of collaborative discussions (one-on-one, in groups, and teacher-led) with diverse partners on grades 9–10 topics, texts, and issues, building on others' ideas and expressing their own clearly and persuasively.
	SL.9-10.1c Propel conversations by posing and responding to questions that relate the current discussion to broader themes or larger ideas; actively incorporate others into the discussion; and clarify, verify, or challenge ideas and conclusions.
	SL.9-10.1d Respond thoughtfully to diverse perspectives, summarize points of agreement and disagreement, and, when warranted, qualify or justify their own views and understanding and make new connections in light of the evidence and reasoning presented.
	W.9-10.4 Produce clear and coherent writing in which the development, organization, and style are appropriate to task, purpose, and audience.
	W.9-10.5 Develop and strengthen writing as needed by planning, revising, editing, rewriting, or trying a new approach, focusing on addressing what is most significant for a specific purpose and audience.
Lesson 10	RI.9-10.1 Cite strong and thorough textual evidence to support analysis of what the text says explicitly as well as inferences drawn from the text..RI.9-10.2 Determine a central idea of a text and analyze its development over the course of the text, including how it emerges and is shaped and refined by specific details; provide an objective summary of the text.
	RI.9-10.3 Analyze how the author unfolds an analysis or series of ideas or events, including the order in which the points are made, how they are introduced and developed, and the connections that are drawn between them.
	RI.9-10.4 Determine the meaning of words and phrases as they are used in a text, including figurative, connotative, and technical meanings; analyze the cumulative impact of specific word choices on meaning and tone (e.g., how the language of a court opinion differs from that of a newspaper).
	RI.9-10.6 Determine an author's point of view or purpose in a text and analyze how an author uses rhetoric to advance that point of view or purpose.
	SL.9-10.1 Initiate and participate effectively in a range of collaborative discussions (one-on-one, in groups, and teacher-led) with diverse partners on grades 9–10 topics, texts, and issues, building on others' ideas and expressing their own clearly and persuasively.
	SL.9-10.1c Propel conversations by posing and responding to questions that relate the current discussion to broader themes or larger ideas; actively incorporate others into the discussion; and clarify, verify, or challenge ideas and conclusions.

Lesson	Common Core State Standards in ELA/Literacy
Lesson 10, *continued*	SL.9-10.1d Respond thoughtfully to diverse perspectives, summarize points of agreement and disagreement, and, when warranted, qualify or justify their own views and understanding and make new connections in light of the evidence and reasoning presented.
	SL.9-10.4 Present information, findings, and supporting evidence clearly, concisely, and logically such that listeners can follow the line of reasoning and the organization, development, substance, and style are appropriate to purpose, audience, and task.
	W.9-10.4 Produce clear and coherent writing in which the development, organization, and style are appropriate to task, purpose, and audience.
	W.9-10.5 Develop and strengthen writing as needed by planning, revising, editing, rewriting, or trying a new approach, focusing on addressing what is most significant for a specific purpose and audience.
Lesson 11	RL.9-10.1 Cite strong and thorough textual evidence to support analysis of what the text says explicitly as well as inferences drawn from the text.
	RL.9-10.2 Determine a theme or central idea of a text and analyze in detail its development over the course of the text, including how it emerges and is shaped and refined by specific details; provide an objective summary of the text.
	RL.9-10.4 Determine the meaning of words and phrases as they are used in the text, including figurative and connotative meanings; analyze the cumulative impact of specific word choices on meaning and tone (e.g., how the language evokes a sense of time and place; how it sets a formal or informal tone).
	SL.9-10.1 Initiate and participate effectively in a range of collaborative discussions (one-on-one, in groups, and teacher-led) with diverse partners on grades 9–10 topics, texts, and issues, building on others' ideas and expressing their own clearly and persuasively.
	SL.9-10.1c Propel conversations by posing and responding to questions that relate the current discussion to broader themes or larger ideas; actively incorporate others into the discussion; and clarify, verify, or challenge ideas and conclusions.
	SL.9-10.1d Respond thoughtfully to diverse perspectives, summarize points of agreement and disagreement, and, when warranted, qualify or justify their own views and understanding and make new connections in light of the evidence and reasoning presented.
	W.9-10.4 Produce clear and coherent writing in which the development, organization, and style are appropriate to task, purpose, and audience.
	W.9-10.5 Develop and strengthen writing as needed by planning, revising, editing, rewriting, or trying a new approach, focusing on addressing what is most significant for a specific purpose and audience.
Lesson 12	Varies based on product choice.